WINSLOW FARM

Charlotte S. Snead

Published by Van Rye Publishing, LLC
www.vanryepublishing.com

Library of Congress Control Number: 2018946379
ISBN-13: 978-0-9982893-2-8
ISBN-10: 0-9982893-2-9

Dedication

To my Forever Love, Dr. Joseph A. Snead.
We married when we were kids and have grown old together.
Fifty-five years later, I'd do it all over again, but a lot better.
Thanks for your constant love and for your never-ending
support in all I have accomplished.

Contents

CHAPTER 1

Joy Arrives

BRIAN TUGGED ON Gabe's sleeve and pointed down the road. A sleek black limo slowed to a stop. Before its driver could move around the car to open the door, a slender leg emerged, and a woman who appeared to be in her early twenties, of medium height with long blonde hair stepped out. As the driver neared her, the woman held out a wad of bills and flashed a brilliant smile. Looking around, she started down the road while the driver returned to his seat. The car eased around her, moving toward Brian and Gabe.

"Who is she?" Brian asked.

"Must be our new owner," Gabe responded.

"I'll be appropriate."

Gabe put an arm around the boy's shoulder. "I know you will, buddy. Good man."

The boy beamed and watched the young woman approach. "She sings." Gabe did not ask how Brian knew this. Sometimes Brian knew things.

The woman meandered down the driveway, enjoying the beautiful summer day. The limo eased to a stop beside them, and the driver rolled down his window. With an easy smile, Gabe

1

greeted him. "I'm the caretaker. I assume that's Ms. Thomas?" The driver bobbed his head in agreement. "Yes, sir. She wanted to walk. I'm taking her bags."

Gabe pointed ahead to the large house at the end of the long driveway. "Set them on the porch and I'll carry them in for her." The driver nodded and moved the car forward. Gabe watched him place six bags on the porch, including one large, long bag that looked heavy. *I wonder how high-maintenance she is.* As the lovely woman approached, they could hear her sweet singing. Gabe nudged his brother. "Right again, Bri. How do you do that?"

With his lopsided grin, Brian replied, "I just know. I'll be appropriate."

"Do you want to meet her? I know you're shy with people you don't know."

"Yeah. She's nice." Brian's sweet face showed eagerness as she approached.

"You just know, right?" With an earnest nod, Brian took a step forward. They both stepped down from the front steps of their small caretaker's cottage set back against the woods, next to the other side of the driveway, about eighty feet from the main house. "Let's go meet her then." Throwing his arm around the boy to provide additional security, Gabe urged him toward the smiling woman who neared them as she waved to the departing limo.

"Welcome to your new home." Gabe said the greeting without grief ravaging his heart. He had accepted this. He had to sell the farm to pay his parents' funeral expenses and settle their debts, mostly medical bills. His dad died instantly in the wreck, but the doctors tried valiantly to save his mom, who died before Gabe arrived almost forty-eight hours later. All Gabe wanted to do by the time he arrived was sleep. The nurse told him they had sedated Brian again minutes before he arrived, so Gabe crashed in the chair beside the bed.

A social worker had appeared within twenty minutes, and she informed Gabe that Brian had entered the hospital covered in their mother's blood. The boy had gotten out of the back seat and crawled in beside her up front. So the hospital kept him under sedation until his brother arrived to care for him—not that he knew Gabe all that well. Gabe had been home on leaves in between assignments, but essentially Brian was raised an only child, being almost twenty years younger than Gabe.

When Gabe got home from Afghanistan on his final leave, he was his brother's only living relative, and he resigned from the military to care for him. Brian, traumatized from the wreck, never entered their house again after a first sleepless night there. He was proud of his soldier brother, and he scrawled him frequent notes, mostly in the form of drawing him pictures. Their mother had sent Brian's school pictures to Gabe every year, and Gabe watched him lose his teeth and grow new ones. Their pastor told Gabe he had promised Brian his brother would be home, and, in and out of his medicated dozing, Brian looked forward to someone familiar.

In the months since their parents' funeral, the brothers had grown close, working side by side. When Brian refused to enter the house, weeping copiously for his mama and dad, Gabe realized they needed to create a new space. He purchased a used camper trailer, and together they built a small caretaker's cottage.

While Brian could not enter the motherless main house, he still loved the farm, and he would be traumatized even further if he lost it as well. So Gabe had come up with the idea of selling the house with an on-site caretaker, and he began working on the cottage. He needed to provide for his brother, and he did not have enough years in the service to be pensioned. The army still wanted him, and it offered a big signing bonus to stay, but Gabe was determined his brother would not face Down syndrome alone. Brian had always been surrounded by his parents' love, and Gabe would fill the void as best he could.

God provided Ms. Thomas to the brothers the month after Gabe put the house on the market, and she accepted the caretaker idea. Apparently, she traveled for her job. After the settlement, Gabe established a trust for the boy. He had not realized how much Brian's care cost his parents. Now Brian was older and was in special education through the school system.

Gabe, his arm tucked securely around his brother's shoulders, met his new boss with a smile and continued his greeting. "We're glad you've arrived. How was your flight from Nashville?"

"It was fine, thank you. This is a beautiful place, isn't it? I remembered the area from when I was a child. That's why I bought it, sight unseen."

"You lived in this area? When?"

"I went to Lost Creek Elementary and the middle school. But when my career started to take off, we moved to Nashville."

Ms. Joy Thomas, famous and rising bluegrass singer. That explains a lot! Gabe glanced over at the six bags awaiting him on the porch. "Shall we get you settled in then? Bri, you want to wait out here? I won't be long, buddy."

Joy turned to the boy. "Come on in, Brian. May I call you Brian? I'm Joy Thomas." Eyes solemn, Brian nodded. "You may call me Joy. And *you* are?" She lifted cornflower blue eyes to

Gabe.

"Forgive me. I'm Gabe Winslow, your caretaker. Let's get your bags inside." Gabe approached the house, and he was startled when Brian trailed along. "So, your flight was okay?"

"Easy peasy," she replied, winking at Brian with none of the awkwardness most people displayed in the face of the lad's obvious disability. She even slipped her arm in his. "Tell me about yourself, young man. Where do you go to school?"

"I go to Lost Creek Elementary, too."

"Oh, we have something in common. That's cool." Joy's arm squeezed his.

Brian looked up at Gabe. "I told you she was nice."

"Brian knows things." Gabe winked at Joy.

"It takes one to know one, Brian. You're nice, too." Joy took Brian's hand as they walked up the steps.

Gabe kept a close eye on his brother. Brian had not been inside the house since the funeral, but, clinging to Joy's hand, he stepped over the threshold. Perhaps Gabe would face the consequences later. For now, he was proud of the lad.

A housekeeper had come before Joy arrived, so the house was spotless. But Gabe did not have the money or time to clean or paint the caretaker's cottage at the same time. "You'll probably want to have the place painted, but I thought you'd like to choose the colors."

Joy looked around, her bright blue eyes sparkling. "Someone loved this place. It's homey and perfect. I love it."

Brian moved closer to Gabe's side, and the older brother again put his arm around the boy. "Gabe loves, and he plays the guitar, and he has wings."

"Wings?" Joy frowned in confusion.

5

Gabe shrugged. "He saw a picture of Gabriel in Mom's Bible, and now he insists I have wings."

"I see them," Brian insisted.

"Okay, buddy."

"I do."

"Not everybody can see what you see, Brian," Joy said in support. She put long, slender fingers on each of his cheeks, tilting his head to meet her eyes. She then looked at Gabe. "It takes an innocent heart."

Waiting for Brian to decompensate over this intimate touch, which never happened, tears sprung to Gabe's eyes. *High-maintenance? I don't think so!* Gabe shook himself—*Not appropriate to cry*—and studied his employer with new eyes. "Where do you want these? Lots of bedrooms upstairs, but the master suite is down here."

"Another reason I bought it. I can bring the whole band here. I'll take the master bedroom. I'm a singer, Brian, and I travel with a band."

"I told you she sings!" Brian crowed.

With a shrug, Gabe led the way, wondering if Brian would follow. Brian's steps slowed as they neared the room, but Gabe and the housekeeper had rearranged it from what Brian remembered. The bed was on a different wall, covered with a new spread, and they had hung matching curtains. Dad's easy chair was also gone, replaced by a love seat. Brian looked around without a word.

"You okay, buddy?" Tears hovered in Brian's eyes, but he was silent, squeezing Gabe's hand. "Let me get the rest of the bags, and we can get out of here, okay?" Brian nodded, and, to Gabe's amazement, he remained with Joy while his big brother left and returned with three more suitcases. "We put enough food in the refrigerator and cabinets, so you can survive until you get to the store. One more little bag, Bri."

"Oh, I can fetch it. You gentlemen have been most kind. Thank you. Does the furniture come with the house?"

"What there is of it, if you want it." Gabe had moved his and Brian's bedroom furniture to the caretaker's cottage, along with the kitchen table and chairs and several living room pieces. "If you want to buy new appliances, we'd take the old ones to the cottage. The washer and dryer are new, though, and we left them for you."

Joy studied him. Gabe figured she realized she was living in their old home, and he bet she wondered why. But she did not ask. "I'm sure I'll be most comfortable here."

"No ghosts," Brian interjected. Gabe looked at him and wondered if that was why his brother had been so upset their first night out of the hospital.

Joy gave Brian an impulsive hug. "Only happy memories, right?"

Seeing the waterworks mounting in Brian, Gabe put his arm around his brother, turned him to the door, and led him out. "You did good, buddy. I'm proud of you."

"I told you she was nice." Tears ran down the boy's face. Gabe handed him a handkerchief, which he had learned to carry because the lad always needed cleaning up. Brian accepted it, and he mopped his own face. "I like having her here."

"She'll fill the place with *joy*, won't she?"

Brian burst into a grin. He got it! "Yeah," he replied. "With joy. With *Joy*-joy."

7

CHAPTER 2

Joy's New Car

GABE HAD LEFT HIS phone number on the kitchen counter of the house, and, after eating breakfast with Brian, they heard his phone ring.

"Are you busy? I mean, you must be, keeping up with 120 acres. But I have a minor problem. Since I left my car in Nashville, I'll have to buy a car to get around here. Could you possibly take me to get one?"

Gabe chuckled. "You're the boss, ma'am. I'm not too busy. I had planned to mow the meadow, but the turkeys are still nesting."

"Oh, we have turkeys? How exciting!"

"You'll see them around. Last week Brian and I saw twelve, and over fifteen yesterday. Whatever you'd like to do is fine. May Bri—"

Before he finished the sentence, Joy rushed on. "And Brian is welcome. Maybe we can stop at Chick-fil-A to get a sandwich and a shake. Wait, I have a call." Gabe waited while she switched to the other call. When she clicked back, she said it was from her publicist's secretary. Some fan had sent a huge bouquet. She told the secretary to enjoy it.

"Does that happen often?" Gabe asked.

She replied that it was a first. "Whoever sent it signed it, 'Your biggest fan.'"

Gabe returned to their conversation. "Chick-fil-A is Brian's favorite stop."

"Mine, too—something else in common."

"When will you be ready?"

"Anytime."

"I'll stack the dishes and be right up."

Brian's face lit up when Gabe told him their plans. "We're going with Joy?"

"We are. As soon as you scrub the eggs and jelly off your face."

"That would be appropriate."

Gabe chuckled. "Very."

"Was I appropriate yesterday?"

Gabe grimaced. "Yeah. Except maybe the comment about ghosts."

"Okay. No ghosts."

"Only happy memories."

"I cried, Gabe. Is it appropriate to cry?"

"Buddy, after all you've been through, it's very appropriate to cry. I cry, too, sometimes."

"You do? Thought soldiers never cry."

Gabe drew his brother into a hug. "Buddy, I never met a soldier who didn't cry."

"Really?"

"Really. Come on; Joy is waiting." The phrase hung in Gabe's thoughts. *Joy is waiting.*

"Is a jacket appropriate?"

Gabe chuckled again. "No, it's warm."

"It's June, right?" Gabe took him to the calendar and pointed. He always did that, showing his brother things.

They left the cottage and crossed the driveway, walking over to their old home. This time, Brian remained on the sidewalk while Gabe climbed the steps and rang the bell.

Joy opened instantly. "Do you have a key?"

Gabe reached into his pocket and handed one to her. "Sorry. I meant to give it to you yesterday. I . . . needed to get Brian home."

"I noticed he was upset."

"It's the first time he's been in the house since Mom and Dad died."

She sniffed. "Oh, I'm sorry. I didn't realize."

"It was good for him. A big step, but tough. He cried a lot. His eyes are still a little red, but we got through it."

Joy turned the key in the door and looked for Brian. Spying him on the sidewalk, she skipped down the stairs. "Hey, Brian." She kissed his cheek, and to Gabe's surprise, he kissed her back.

"Hey, that's not fair! It took me three months to get a kiss."

Brian bowed his head. "I love you, Gabe."

"I love you, too, little brother. It took some time for us to get to know one another, didn't it?" He turned to Joy. "I'd been in Afghanistan for eight months before I came home."

"Soldiers cry, too, Joy. Did you know that? Even big, brave soldiers like Gabe."

"God gives us tears, Brian. He collects them in a jar in heaven. I ought to write a song about that."

"You *write* songs, too?"

"Sure do."

"Gabe plays the guitar."

10

"And he loves. I didn't forget. And he has wings, but I haven't seen them yet."

"You wanna ride in Gabe's truck?"

"Oh, he has *wheels*, too?"

Brian giggled. Looking at his sparkling eyes, Gabe wondered if Joy was magic. Where was the boy who cried himself to sleep in his brother's strong arms the night before?

"Show her the stream, Gabe."

"Come on, dude, you didn't show me that for a month!" Gabe put his arm on the seatback and tousled the boy's raven hair. Brian giggled. "Okay, I will."

Gabe backed the truck up and continued down the road, past the barn. They bumped along for about a mile, pulling over beside a gurgling stream. Before the truck was completely stopped, Joy was out the door. "Oh, how beautiful! I love it. Does it have fish?"

"Lots and lots," Brian assured her, hopping out of the truck and taking her hand.

Gabe followed the exuberant pair more slowly. "Some of them are even big enough to keep."

"If they are smaller than this," Brian held up his hands about eight inches apart, "you have to throw them back."

"Will you teach me?"

"Gabe can. He's good."

"Oh, I can't wait!"

"We'll have to consider that when we choose a car. What do you want?" Gabe prodded. Joy paused, thinking. "Well, what do you have in Nashville?"

She giggled. "I can tell you it won't get me around the farm. A Prius."

Gabe bit back laughter. "You need a four-wheel drive around here. A small truck or a Jeep. Sometimes the stream comes up quickly."

"Let's go look at a Jeep."

Gabe backed up again, and they bumped back past the house and down the long driveway, turning onto the main road. "Did your driver have trouble finding the place?"

"He had a GPS. And the realtor sent a map."

Gabe grunted. "We used to be off the grid. I liked that better."

"Why? Are you a recluse?"

"I'm a soldier."

Within a half an hour they were at the Jeep dealer. They walked around the showroom, and Joy asked Brian about the color.

"I want it to be safe. You gotta be safe," Brian insisted. The salesman broke into all the newest safety features, but Brian frowned and fretted. "Can you keep her safe, Gabe?"

"Life is never completely safe, Bri. But we can wear our seatbelts and drive carefully."

"Mama and Dad had their seatbelts on, and Dad was a good driver." Brian's voice began to escalate in mounting panic. Gabe drew him over to the side, whispering, while the salesman shifted his feet.

Joy leaned in toward the salesman, saying in a confidential voice, "I think his parents died in an automobile wreck."

"That truck came out of *nowhere*, Gabe!" Gabe steered Brian to a nearby chair, pushing his hair back and holding him close. He continued to whisper, and he pulled a handkerchief out of his pocket to wipe the boy's eyes with a gentle touch.

Finally, Brian stood and approached Joy and the salesman. "I like the blue one, Joy. It matches your beautiful eyes."

Leaning beside it, she fluttered her eyelashes and asked, "Do you think so?"

Brian walked back to Gabe. "Was that appropriate?"

"That was honest, buddy. She does have beautiful blue eyes."

Joy blushed. *So, she's still unspoiled. I hope she stays that way.* Gabe watched while the vehicle was selected, and he suggested they leave and come back for it. Checking his watch, he asked the salesman what time they should return.

"Since she's writing a check for the entire amount, why don't all of you go to lunch and come back say . . . around noon?"

Brian and Joy gave each other a high five. Gabe rolled his eyes and pushed the two of them out the door. "Get out of here, you two."

As they approached the restaurant, Gabe reminded the boy that the play area was not appropriate for a ten-year-old. "He has a hard time grasping that," he explained to Joy.

"I can understand. It's fun, but a big boy like you could sit on a little kid's hand and break it."

"That's what Gabe said. But I still like Chick-fil-A. It has good music and good food. It's my favorite. I'll be appropriate."

"What is this 'appropriate' deal?"

"It's his latest word."

"Gabe said I had to be appropriate, or you wouldn't want us to be your caretakers. We want to be your caretakers."

"Oh, I *need* a caretaker. I wouldn't know how to take care of a farm, and I can't imagine being there without you. You belong there. You have to show me all your favorite places on the farm."

"I told you she was nice. Is that appropriate?"

Joy gave a merry laugh and hugged Brian. "I consider that a

most appropriate compliment."

Sitting in the restaurant, sipping on their shakes and munching their sandwiches, one of Joy's songs came on. Brian recognized it because she sang it coming down the road the previous day, and he commented on it. She confirmed it was one of her songs, but she asked him to be quiet and keep her secret. Brian was excited and began to bounce in his seat and swing his legs. Gabe reached over and patted his leg to settle him.

After they ate, they went to nearby Kohl's to buy some jeans for the growing boy. Hoping against hope Brian would not throw a tantrum, Gabe asked, "Do we need to go over what's appropriate in Kohl's?"

"I hate to shop."

"I know. Your pants are getting to be high-waters, but we can come back another time."

"I want to help. Come on, Brian." Joy handled Brian like a pro, explaining why this pair was too small, and that one was too big. She even convinced him to try them on—much easier than Gabe and Brian's usual mode of taking them home and returning them.

"You're good with him."

"I like him. Kids can sense that."

"He's hard on strangers. Every year, it took Mom a month to get him used to a new teacher."

"He's a sweetie," Joy replied.

They stopped by Walgreens to pick up something Joy forgot, with Gabe and Brian waiting in the car. "Mama said sometimes ladies need to get personal stuff and guys shouldn't come."

"Sure, Bri."

"Did you know that, Gabe?"

14

"Sounds about right."

"Yep. Here she comes!"

"Now to pick up my car," Joy said, getting back into the truck.

When they arrived at the dealership, the car was sitting outside, shining and bright. The salesman met Joy and handed her the keys, leaning in to point out a few things.

Gabe led the way home next to Brian, who kept looking back to see whether Joy was safe as she followed them in her new car. Noticing his lips moving, Gabe realized he was praying. "She'll be fine, buddy." The boy rubbed his hand under his nose, and Gabe knew he was crying. How could he help him? It had been six months, and Brian's pain and anxiety seemed as difficult as ever. Then he remembered his own night sweats over battlefield incidents, his parents' wreck, and the little boy covered in his mother's blood. It would take time.

"Daddy told me you'd come home, Gabe."

"I think that was Pastor Davis who told you."

"No. One night in the dark, Daddy came. He told me not to worry. He said you were coming, and the next day, you came."

"I'm glad I came home, Bri." A small sigh escaped the boy's lips, and Gabe thought, even though he had been up for major, nothing could be more rewarding than this little fellow. "I love you lots, buddy. Lots and lots."

"To the moon and back."

"Mama used to say that."

Again, the little sigh. "Yeah, I miss her."

"Me, too, buddy. Me, too."

They turned into the driveway, and Joy was close behind. Brian made sure of that as they continued to the cottage, tooting a farewell salute. Gabe explained they had to give her some space but they would see her again soon. Every hour on the hour, Brian asked him if this was "soon," and Gabe explained again that she had other things to do.

About five o'clock, the phone rang, and Brian ran to answer. "Hello, Brian speaking." He yelled at Gabe, "She said that was appropriate!"

"Don't break her eardrums, buddy." Gabe listened to them as Brian lowered his voice and chatted with their new neighbor. *Maybe she is magic.* Brian hung up without calling him to the phone. "What did she want?"

"She thanked me for her car and said she felt very safe. And she said she has too much food and wants us to come to the house for dinner. But then she said if it was better, she could come here. It's better. She's coming at six and bringing it."

"Wow, she said all that?" Brian bobbed his head. "Okay. We need to pick up the place a bit. And do you want to take a bath before she comes?"

Brian lifted his arm and sniffed. "I don't stink."

Gabe laughed. Brian did what he did after a hard day's work. "No, you don't. Let's play fish." The card game was an easy way to teach him numbers.

Soon, a tap came at the door, and Brian ran to open it. Joy struggled with a big basket, which Gabe took from her hands and set on the counter. He started to scoop up the game, but she gave a mock pout and said, "How could you play fish without me?"

"One quick hand and more after dinner. That smells too good to wait."

Joy looked around. "This cottage is brand new."

"We builded it. Gabe and me." Brian hung his head. "It's be-

16

cause I couldn't go in the house. Mama didn't die there. She died in the hospital. But I got blood all over me."

Gabe could not believe what he was hearing. His brother never shared all that before, although Gabe knew about it—the social worker and the nurses had told him about it. He wiped his eyes.

Joy knelt beside the boy's chair and took him in her arms. "Oh, Brian, you were so brave for your mother. Did you see Jesus? Jesus said when we die He comes for us and receives us to Himself. Jesus came to take your mama to heaven."

"Maybe I did. It was a big light." Now Gabe's tears were running down his face. "Don't cry, Gabe. Jesus was there. That's cool. And now your wings are glowing."

To give them privacy, Joy had turned her back and begun serving. She poured Brian a glass of milk and made herself ice water. "What do you want to drink, Gabe?"

"Water's good."

Gabe sat on his chair, and Brian snuggled in his lap. "Bri, you are a gift from God, buddy."

"Joy is our gift from God," Brian responded.

"That, too." Gabe lifted his head. "Thanks."

"Thank you two. I visited heaven tonight, even though I lost my hand of fish."

They laughed. Gabe pushed Brian up to the table, tucking a napkin into his shirt. He held a chair for Joy before circling to his own. He started the prayer but could not finish, so Joy took it up, thanking God for this food, this family, and the knowledge of heaven where Brian's mom and dad waited for him and Gabe.

"Mama always worried Gabe would die in the war. I heard her cry and pray. And Dad prayed, too. But Gabe came home to stay with me, and he's not going back over there. Ever. Right,

Gabe?"

"No, Bri, you're stuck with me."

A brilliant smile lit Brian's face. "I'm glad."

"Me, too, buddy. Me, too."

The rest of dinner lightened up. Joy told stories about her younger sisters' escapades and had them all laughing around the table.

"Thanks for dinner, Joy. It's the best meal we've had in ages."

"Gabe is a good brother, but he don't cook so good."

"Doesn't, Bri."

"Doesn't. Except breakfast. He can cook breakfast real good. But the rest of the time we eat hot dogs and canned psghetti."

"You'd better stop. Joy will think we're begging."

"Oh. That's not appropriate, is it?"

"Nope." Gabe stood, clearing plates and putting them in the sink. "But I can dish up ice cream. I have fudge royal, chocolate chip, and vanilla." He scooped up a dish of each and asked Joy her plans for the next day. She planned to go grocery shopping, and she asked his plans.

"Brian and I are going to clean up the barn." Seeing the boy's scowl, he added, "We're going to work hard and have fun."

"What kind of animals are we going to get?" Joy asked.

"None, if we can't get the barn clean."

"Can we get goats?"

Gabe chuckled. "Lady, this is your place, but nannies need milking, and Billy goats stink to high heaven. Some ponies are fun, but they poop, and that must be cleaned up, too."

"My sisters would love ponies."

"Will they shovel? Let's think on it a while."

"I thought we were caretakers."

Gabe raised his eyebrows. "You want to clean up the barn to have animals, Bri?"

"Maybe."

"No maybe about it. Animals require work and commitment."

"Can I have a dog, Gabe? Can I?"

"Let's see how you do cleaning up the barn, and I'll think about it."

Putting her dish in the sink, Joy said, "I've had a wonderful day, but all good things must come to an end."

"The housekeeper comes tomorrow. Do you want to keep her?"

"Yes. I need to get the house ready—the band is coming in next week."

Knowing that would be a problem for Brian, Gabe followed her out. "Brian has done exceptionally well with you, but he is shy, and . . ." His voice trailed off.

"So, we should introduce strangers slowly?"

"You are intuitive, and it's your place." He shrugged. "I'll keep him with me."

"I love Brian, Gabe. I'll prepare the guys and see how it goes."

"He's put on a good show for you, but he isn't always easy." Gabe ran his hand down his face.

"It'll work out, Gabe. You'll see." Joy stood on tiptoe and kissed his cheek. "'Night."

CHAPTER 3

Joy

JOY ALREADY LOVED this place, far from the noise and clamor of Nashville. She loved her music, but she hated the acclaim and publicity. She drew a deep breath of fresh mountain air, remembering that to the locals, these were not mountains, only hills. But she was home.

She went through the house and slid a door in her bedroom open to step out onto the back deck. She claimed a seat on the swing there, and she pushed it off with her feet, looking up at the darkening sky. She had fun with Gabe and Brian, and she thought about them, finding it difficult to believe she had only known them two days.

Humming to herself, Joy looked up, seeing the bright stars, the big dipper, and Venus. The night was cool, and she drew her sweater around her, thankful she had picked it up in the bedroom. She had remembered it cooled off at night in West Virginia. She liked it here and knew she had made the right decision coming back. New songs were already popping up in her head—a song about Jesus, coming for his own, and fish splashing in the stream. *Wasn't there a fish in the night sky? Oh, yes—Pisces.*

She closed her eyes, feeling the night breeze kiss her cheeks, and she smiled, thinking of Brian being "appropriate" and Gabe's patient gentleness with him. How had he learned that? He said they had not been together much as children because he was gone most of the time. Figuring Brian was about ten—he was born after she moved away—that meant Gabe was probably thirty. She wondered why twenty years lay between the brothers.

Since Joy had left in middle school, she tried to remember Gabe from around that time. Maybe she had a vague idea of him being on the high school football team, as she must be six or seven years younger. Then she remembered write-ups in the paper. She thought Gabe had gotten an ROTC scholarship to Virginia Tech. Hearing her phone ring, she went inside.

"Are you all right?" Gabe asked. "I didn't see any lights on in the house."

"I'm sitting on the back deck, trying to remember you. Didn't you play football and go to Virginia Tech on an ROTC scholarship?"

"Not too memorable, was I? Funny, you think you're such a hot-shot when you get a letter. You're right—I did go to Tech. But you must have been in middle school."

"Even less memorable. I was in show choir."

"You're memorable now."

"Thank you, I guess. You're sweet with Brian. How did you learn to be so patient?"

"It takes incredible patience to be a sniper."

"You were a sniper?"

"Hunted all my life. It came naturally. But it's a lot different killing a man."

She was quiet. "How did you do it?"

He took a deep breath. "When you see someone mowing

down your buddies, killing them in cold blood, it's not too hard. I remember one guy on a rooftop. He killed six of my guys before I got him. You want to take them out, to stop the carnage."

"Oh."

"But I'm glad to be out of it. I love my brother. I was amazed what he shared tonight. His psychologist will be thrilled to hear it."

"He has a psychologist?"

"He had a traumatic experience. The psychologist works with special ed kids. The hospital had to sedate him until I got home. I got here within forty-eight hours, and then we had to get to know each other. Dr. Wells was a big help with that."

"You guys are close now."

"It took a lot of work, but I wouldn't trade it for the world. He's a precious kid. Special."

"And you are a tender man."

"That kid makes mush out of me. I see your lights on now. Are you okay over there by yourself? I'm sorry about the ghost comment, by the way. I told him it wasn't appropriate. That might be why he explained how Mom died. Maybe he felt he should tell you."

"I feel no ghost—only a lot of love in this house."

"Yep, a lot of love. Mom always wanted a bunch of kids. That's why they had all the bedrooms. But it didn't happen, so they took in foster kids, and then they finally had Brian. They were older when he was born, but he was loved unconditionally."

"I can tell. And you were, too."

"Yep. The best parents in the world. This sucks. I hate that Brian won't have them."

"But he has you. What time does the housekeeper come?"

"Yeah, he has me. Nine."

22

"'Night again."

* * *

In the morning, Joy learned from the housekeeper how she and Gabe had rearranged the parents' bedroom. He had been worried about Brian, so they did it while the boy was at the psychologist. Joy marveled again at Gabe's tender concern. And Jolene, the housekeeper, told Joy about the brothers' only night in the house when they returned from the hospital and why they moved out of it. "Gabe went out the next day and rented a small trailer and started building the cottage so they could stay on the farm."

Joy needed two more beds for an empty room. But she told Jolene to change the linens in the rest of the house in preparation for the band coming. Jolene's face clouded at the news about the band.

"Gabe told me Brian is shy, so we'll take it slow with the band here. We have five guys in the band, and all of them are good guys. Gabe said he's done exceptionally well with me, and I'm glad for that."

"Did he tell you Gabe has wings?"

Joy grinned. "He did."

"I wouldn't doubt it," Jolene added. "I've seen him hold that child while he trembled when anyone new came by. He's scared, Miss Joy. He's not a bad boy, Brian, but he's scared of his own shadow. But I've seen a big difference since Mr. Gabe's been here."

After the ladies agreed the sheets were fine, Joy still needed to buy the new beds, so she set off. While her new friend worked, Joy went to the store, getting groceries, as well as supplies Jolene had requested. She had wondered about the extra beds upstairs, but now she understood—it was because of the foster kids. She noticed Gabe's truck was not there when she left, but by the time she got back, he was home. Seeing her struggling with the groceries, he jogged across the lawn and driveway to help.

"Where's Brian?" Joy wondered.

"He's asleep. Today we went to see the psychologist, and sometimes he's pretty tuckered out when he's done. He's made significant progress, though. And, like I said, Dr. Wells was impressed with what he told you. Thank you for that. What else do you have?"

"I can get the Kmart bags, thanks. We need to wash and replace two spreads once I get two more beds, but the sheets are fine. Jolene should have them in the dryer now. Do you need to wash?"

"I bought a stack washer and dryer for the cottage. So we're all set, but thanks. Anything else?"

"Nope. I'm good. Thanks for your help."

Gabe heard the shrieks before she did, and he ran to the house, throwing open the door and gathering Brian in his arms. The door closed behind them, and Joy murmured a prayer before entering the house.

Jolene helped Miss Joy unpack the groceries and told her Gabe does not let Brian have Oreo cookies because they "sugar him up" but that he does like sugar cookies. So Joy made up a batch, planning to take them over to the cottage after lunch. Joy asked Jolene how much Gabe had paid her and then wrote her out a check and another to reimburse him. She asked Jolene if she could work extra when the band came, and she bid her good-day about three o'clock.

When Joy called about coming down to the caretaker's cottage, Gabe told her it was not a good time. He and Brian were reading, coming down from his emotional morning. "Maybe later, though."

Joy took a cup of coffee to her front porch, looking across at the cottage set back against the woods. Setting her cup on a table, she prayed for Brian, weeping. She went back inside to get the pencil and the pad of paper she always kept close at hand, and she began to jot lyrics about Jesus coming to receive us to himself.

Joy had fallen into a good thing at Winslow Farm. Her caretakers were . . . "scrumptious" was the word that came to mind. Maybe Gabe had been in high school when she was at South Harrison middle, but six or seven years did not matter too much at this age, did it? And Brian was . . . he was special, like Gabe said. Her mouth curved as she wondered about a song called "Gabriel Has Wings." Like Jolene, she could easily imagine it if only she had the boy's innocent eyes.

She heard the brothers before she spotted them. Brian was subdued but talking. "Are you sure?" she heard him ask.

"I'm sure. She called and said she made them especially for you."

"For me? Mama made me cookies, too."

Joy called out, "I'm on the back deck." *Maybe the boy was overcome by emotions again. How did Gabe know what to do? He always said the right things. But he said it took time. God, help me.*

"Hi, guys," she said in a bright voice, poking her head around the corner. "Do you want to come around?" *Score one. She spared Brian another trip through the bedroom.*

"I told Brian you made him cookies, so we came to snatch one."

"I made them for you, Brian. And if you're a good boy, Gabe, maybe I'll let you have a few, too. Come sit. I'll bring them out. Want a glass of milk, too?"

"Yes, please."

"That was appropriate, Brian. I'll be right back. Take a seat." She slipped into the house, returning with a plate of cookies and three glasses of milk on a tray. Gabe stood to help her with the door. He had placed two more chairs beside Joy's, and he had moved a table into the middle, where she set the tray. "Okay, dig in. I can't eat all those—I'd be fat as a pig!"

Gabe looked her over. "Don't think so, do you, Bri?"

Brian giggled. "She's skinny. Oops, I guess that's not appropriate."

Gabe laughed. "Ladies always like to hear that."

Joy added, "Except anorexics, but I've never been accused of that."

"No, I guess not, and that's a good thing."

"She's perfect."

"Thank you, Brian. That's a good thing, too—very appropriate."

Brian grinned at Gabe, who winked at him after he reached for another cookie. Gabe shoved the plate toward the boy. "I'd better stop, too, or I'll lose my girlish figure."

"You aren't girlish, Gabe. You're a guy."

He winked at Joy. "Yep, last time I checked."

An image of checking out his guy figure flashed in Joy's head, and she blushed. Fortunately, Brian chattered on. "'Sides, he runs almost every day, and I can't keep up with him on my bike. And I ride fast, too!"

"You do, buddy. We go to the rails-to-trails beside the Mount

26

Clare Road, as far as he can ride. And he's up to six or seven miles now. We stop and rest, then turn back to get the truck, which we park in a church parking lot."

"Where do you go to church?"

"I go to Quiet Dell Methodist. Their pastor understands Brian, and the congregation is very accepting."

"But I'm getting more appropriate, right?"

"Right, buddy."

"You wanna come with us, Joy? It starts at ten o'clock. Both the big hand and the little hand are on the ten, but we leave before then, so we won't be late. What time do we leave, Gabe?"

"About 9:30."

"I take a bath the night before. You should do that, too."

"So I won't be late, right?" Joy agreed. "I'll be standing at the door at 9:25."

Brian frowned. "Is that right, Gabe? You said 9:30."

"That's five minutes early—so she won't be late."

"Oh, that's right. Dad said Mama always forgot something. Don't forget your Bible, Joy."

"I'll set it out the night before, after I read it, of course."

"Gabe reads the Bible to me every night."

"It helps us sleep, doesn't it, Bri? We read Psalm 23, or Psalm 91, and we remember God watches over us every night."

"And we read the Blesseds, too, sometimes."

"The Beatitudes. We sure do."

"Blessed are the pure in heart, for they shall see God," Joy quoted.

Gabe stood. "Are you ready to go, Bri?"

"No."

He chuckled. "That's Brian—ruthlessly honest."

27

"What does that mean?"

"It means you always tell the truth, buddy."

"That's good, isn't it?"

"Almost always, but sometimes it's not appropriate."

"Once I told this lady she was fat. Gabe said it wasn't appropriate."

"It was true, however." Gabe winked at Joy and offered his hand for Brian to take.

The brothers stepped off the porch, and Brian turned back three times to wave. Joy returned the wave each time, and each time Brian pointed it out, enthusiastically. She blew him a kiss and heard him announce in a loud voice, "She blew me a kiss, Gabe!" Gabe turned and gave her a small salute before pulling the boy to his side and challenging him to a race. They sped to their cottage, and they both waved again before they closed the door.

Joy watched them, marveling again at the pair. She thought perhaps Gabe was flirting with her, but, looking back, it was Brian who had pronounced her "perfect." Joy had been so busy building her career—writing songs, recording, and making appearances—that she felt like this was the first time she had taken a break. She sat humming a tune to the lyrics she was working on. "When Jesus returns for us, we will hold His hand, and He will take us." She put her hands to her face. *When You come, Lord, will Brian be perfect?* Then she thought, *He's pretty perfect now, and I bet God is well pleased with him. And with Gabe, too.* God gave her no argument.

CHAPTER 4

The First Band Member Arrives

AFTER CHURCH, THEY went out to lunch. Gabe wondered who should pay. Joy was his boss, but he was the guy. Chick-fil-A was closed, so they went to McDonald's, and Gabe paid. His Social Security survivor's check for Brian was coming in that week, and Brian had a small disability check as well. It was not much, and not enough to live on, but it helped. When they had signed the contract on the house, Joy listed his duties as caretaker, and he agreed to her generous salary. Her reimbursement check for Jolene was unexpected. And he still had savings—a guy could not spend much in Afghanistan.

"Do you have a bike, Joy?" Brian wanted to know. "If you do, we could ride the trail."

"She can ride Mom's. I won't run today; I'll be riding Dad's."

Between the Jeep and the truck, they got their bikes to the church and unloaded them. They had ridden about a mile when a female about Joy's age came upon them and squealed. She had known Joy in show choir, and Gabe took Brian on ahead while they chatted.

The guys eventually circled back, meeting Joy as she approached them. She said the woman had all but ignored her in middle school but was now excited about her career. Joy did not seem too eager to talk about it, so they pedaled along.

As they rode along, Gabe averted his eyes from Joy's strong, athletic legs. He had assumed Ms. Thomas was going to be older, maybe a widow—boy, was he wrong! When Brian asked him about marrying Joy, he explained one does not marry his boss, it is not appropriate. No matter how hard the boy insisted, Gabe stuck to his guns. Brian pouted over that, but Gabe assumed the subject was closed. He hoped so, because now the idea stuck in his mind. She was gorgeous, of course. But she was also kind, and so sweet to Brian. She was the first girl he was attracted to in a long time, and she lived in his head.

They talked about the beautiful day. Gabe commented about needing rain, and Brian announced he was tired. Gabe pointed to a rest area, so they pulled off. Brian pulled petals off a flower, chanting, "She loves me, she loves me not," and then shouted excitedly, "She loves me!"

"Do you have a girlfriend, Brian?"

"No, but neither does . . ." Gabe cleared his throat and raised his eyebrows. "Oh, yeah."

Gabe helped Brian along on his bike, and he cruised on his own, confident Joy could keep up.

"I'll be appropriate, Gabe."

"You almost messed up there, buddy."

"Yeah."

Gabe surged ahead, leaving Brian and Joy in the dust. They did not lose sight of him, however, and he circled back to ride beside them, wiping his sleeve across his brow and commenting on the heat. Gabe thought he was the only one feeling uncomfortable, but when they arrived back at the house, Joy asked to talk to him, and she helped him put the bikes in the barn while Brian gathered flowers.

"What's up?" Gabe asked.

"One of the guys is coming in tomorrow. Willy plays the drums. He loves kids, and I told him about Brian. He's okay with it. Says he'll tell the others."

"Like you said, we'll see how it goes. Brian's so enamored with you, it might be fine. On the other hand, he can be quite possessive."

"Will you talk to him?"

"I will, but no promises. I can't ever predict Brian."

"I wouldn't hurt him for anything. If I need to, we'll rent a place to practice."

"You were planning to work at the house?"

"Yeah. Jolene and I made room in the basement."

"Whatever."

"Just whatever?"

"Joy, it's your house. He's my brother, and I'll deal with it."

"I hate it when you do that!"

"When have I ever done that?"

"I knew you would. I could see that shrug." She waved her hand. "That one."

"What am I supposed to do, Joy?"

"Let me help."

"You want to talk to him?"

"Yes."

"Sure."

They locked the bikes and walked to the cottage. Brian shoved a mangled bunch of wildflowers into Joy's hands, and she exclaimed as if they were hothouse roses. Gabe poured cold lemonade and waved them to the table. Brian looked from one of them to the other.

"Good lemonade."

"Gabe makes good lemonade."

"And good breakfast, right?" Joy took Brian's hand. "You know I'm a singer, don't you, Brian?"

"Yep. You sing good. Did you hear her in church, Gabe?"

"I did. Definitely good."

Joy cleared her throat. "But I do better if I practice, especially to learn new songs. And I have some friends who help me. One of them is coming to see me tomorrow."

"Oh. Are you going to marry him?"

"No. This is work. We work together. He plays the drums. And another guy plays the guitar, and one guy plays the fiddle and flute, and another the banjo and mandolin. And me, of course, I sing."

"All of those people are coming?"

"No, only one guy. The rest will come later. Only Willy to-morrow. Willy likes kids. I told him about you, and he's looking forward to meeting you."

"Did you tell him I'm . . . different?"

"I told him you are very special and that I love you."

"You do?"

"I do."

"That's good, isn't it, Gabe?"

"It's good."

Joy kissed the boy on the cheek and stood. "Thanks for anoth-er lovely day. I'd better get in a hot tub and soak these legs or I'll be stiff tomorrow."

Gabe looked away and stifled a groan. "Then we'll see you

tomorrow. What time will he be in?"

"It's a nine-hour drive, and he's not an early riser. Maybe you'll meet him on Tuesday instead."

"Okay," Brian said. "But maybe not."

"Goodnight, Gabe."

"'Night, Joy. It went all right. But he needs time to process."

Joy walked across the yard. Once again, she reviewed her day with the man and boy who had already come to mean so much to her. She lowered her head. "God, please help Brian with this. Help him to like Willy, and help Willy to reach out to him. Let this be a good thing, God."

She got up and paced the porch, back and forth, wringing her hands. "You led me here, Lord." She felt a breeze and a drop of rain. The temperature had dropped, and the sky darkened. Gabe said they needed rain. Was this a sign? The wind picked up, lifting her blonde hair. Lightning struck nearby, but she was not afraid. She liked storms, especially summer storms. She and her grandmother often used to sit on the back porch and watch them together. Soon, however, the storm drove her inside, coming down harder.

Joy turned lights on, wondering if Gabe was watching. She put her sweater on and closed the sliding door to the deck off her bedroom. The rain lashed the door, and the next bolt of lightning took out the lights. She had not thought to buy candles, but she had a flashlight. While she looked for it, she heard a noise, and the lights flickered back on—some of them. Her bedroom lights, and the master bath lights, but not in the hall. Kitchen lights on. Refrigerator on.

Gabe called on the phone. "I heard the generator come on. We have no lights here, but you should be okay. This is quite a storm."

"You said we need the rain."

"Yeah, but this is too hard. The ground is dry, and it bounces off. Come here, buddy."

"Is Brian okay?"

"Just scared." She heard the boy's voice, and Gabe corrected, "Maybe a little nervous. Let me know if you need anything. The refrigerator should be working."

"It is. Thanks, Gabe."

"We're going to pop some popcorn. Your stove is gas, but you might need to light it with a match."

"Okay."

She did love a storm, and she stood at the door, looking outside as the lightning streaked across the sky. Grandma would have loved this, too. She crossed her arms in front of her chest and could almost feel the old lady beside her. She thought of more lyrics for her song. She would see her grandmother again, as surely as Brian would see his mom and dad. She grabbed her notebook and scribbled some words, humming a tune. It was going to be a good song! Her phone rang again, and she saw it was Willy.

"Hey, girl. I started out early this afternoon, but it's raining hard, so I'm going to pull over and eat. Maybe it will ease up."

"You stop if you need to. I'll pay your hotel bill."

"You must think your song moved up in the charts."

"Last time I checked, it's doing okay."

"Okay?! Did you see the latest? You're about to break a hundred thousand downloads. You're a star baby, and I'm hitching my wagon. Don't write any songs without me."

"Sorry, I'm working on one Brian gave me."

"Brian? The kid you told me about? Wait, I'm turning into a Shoney's."

They talked while he ate dinner. Joy told him how Brian's mother had died in his arms. Willy had the right amount of sympathy for a ten-year-old Down's kid facing something like that. He thought it must be hard for anyone to have his mom die in his arms, let alone a ten-year-old kid with Down's. Joy assured him he would love this innocent boy who "just knows things," and Willy said he looked forward to meeting him.

Peering out the door, Joy said the rain was slowing, and she thought it was coming from the west, so maybe it would slow down for Willy, too. Hearing him order another coffee, she let him go, reminding him it was an hour later here. As the rain eased, the sky began to lighten, although it was still dusk. She whispered a prayer for Willy's safety, and she turned on the outside floodlights.

She was restless, fretting about Brian, praying for him to like Willy. She loved her drummer, but they did not have many black people in this part of West Virginia. Maybe she should have told the boy Willy is black. Then she reproached herself for not trusting God. Surely Brian would love Willy. Willy was a hoot—everybody loved him.

Wandering into the living room, she clicked on the TV. She watched a made-for-TV movie, with the usual story—boy meets girl, they have problems, they work out problems, and they live happily ever after. She thought of Gabe. *Wouldn't that be nice?* She leaned back, replaying scenes in her head, from the movie and from the past week. Before she knew it, she was asleep.

Joy woke up three hours later, groggy, and rubbed her eyes. *Where did Willy say he was? On the other side of Huntington.*

She looked at her watch. *He should be here soon.* She had sent him the directions the realtor gave her, and she told him to call. All the lights had come on, and she fixed a pot of coffee and poured herself a cup, wishing she had not sent the cookies home with Brian and Gabe. She carried her cup to the bathroom and set it on the counter while she brushed out her sleep-tangled hair, shaking the blonde curls out. She brushed her teeth but did not prepare for bed yet. Surely Willy would be there soon.

She had not pulled the drapes, and she saw the van turn in. Going to the front hall, she blinked the overhead lights on and off, and she opened the door, stepping out onto the front porch. She sent Gabe a text, letting him know her friend was coming in, before greeting Willy with an enthusiastic smile. He took the steps two at a time, and she wrapped her arms around his neck, pecking his cheek.

"Love you, girl, but show me the bed," Willy said.

She pointed down the hall. "My room is down there, but yours is upstairs."

Grabbing his suitcase, Willy followed her. "I get first pick. How many bedrooms did they have?"

"Five, counting mine. They had foster kids."

Willy grunted. "Only the good die young. What a shame. The world needs more people like them. I was a foster kid, you know, after my mom died. Saved my life. I'll take this one—faces south. Don't want the eastern sun disturbing my beauty rest."

"I made coffee."

"I had some in Charleston. Now I want sleep."

"I'm glad you're here, Willy, and I hope you get to meet Brian tomorrow. He's shy, and he wasn't expecting to meet you until Tuesday. You finished your gig?"

"Yep."

"I put towels out in the bathroom for you. It's two doors down on the left."

"'Night, gorgeous."

"'Night, crazy man."

Willy already filled the place with himself. He was small—skinny, as Brian would say—but full of love and laughter. *He seriously needs to do something with those dreadlocks, though!* She chuckled to herself, and, after clicking on the nightlight in the hall bathroom upstairs, she went downstairs.

Once in her room, Joy realized the long nap she took earlier made it impossible to sleep. Remembering what Gabe said, she picked up her Bible and read some Psalms. Good old King David—he was tight with God. Even after he sinned, he turned to God with his whole heart. After reading for an hour or so, she turned out the light and prayed a while. She felt peace. Everything was going to be fine—she knew it.

CHAPTER 5

Brian Meets Willy

"COME ON, GABE, let's go. I want to get there before he comes so I can see Joy."

"I told you, he's already here."

"But you explained what early riser means. And he sleeps in." Brian impatiently waved his hand.

"Can't I finish my coffee?"

"No, no, *no!*"

Brian grabbed his brother's hand and dragged him to the door. He looked out the open door and saw a man at the house. At least, he thought it was a man. Brian slowed his steps, but advanced, staring at the man. The man was sitting on the porch step, head down with a coffee cup beside him, steam curling out of it. As they neared, he raised his head. "You must be my man Brian."

"What happened to your hair?"

"You've never seen dreadlocks before?"

"It's sticking up all over the place."

"Joy told me I must do something with this dreadful hair. Isn't she a nag?"

"No. She's *not* a nag!"

"We don't say a negative word about Joy. She loves, and she

sings. Like an angel," Gabe warned the stranger.

Willy stood. "And you're Gabe." He reached out his hand, but even standing on the top step, he barely reached Gabe's shoulders.

"What can you do with your dreadful hair?" Brian persisted.

"Oh, my man, I'd have to wash it and then spend hours combing it out and then braid it in these tiny braids. My mama could do it so fast her fingers flew."

"Where is she?"

"She died, when I was about your age. You're ten?"

Brian nodded his head. "Did she die in a wreck? My Mama did."

"No, she died of an OD."

"I'll explain it to you later, Bri."

"I'd cut it off."

"My hair?"

"Yep. It's really awful."

Willy busted up, leaning at the waist and slapping his knee. "But your brother there, he doesn't have *any* hair."

"It's a military cut. He's a soldier. But it doesn't take any time at all. He just showers. You really ought to cut it. It's easy. I came to see Joy."

"She's inside. Want some coffee, Gabe?"

"More than anything. I can't begin to tell this kid how inappropriate he is."

"He's being honest."

"Always. Ruthlessly."

"It's refreshing."

Hearing the laughter and voices, Joy stepped out onto the porch, asking if they had met. Brian waved his hand. "This little man is Willy. Willy with the dreadful hair."

Biting back a smile, she said, "I told you, Willy. You need to do something with that hair. But you said, 'No, it's too much work.'"

"Brian says I should cut it off, like Gabe's. What do you think?"

"Now?"

"He wouldn't have to wash it and comb it and braid it," Brian reasoned.

"Can I have some of that?" Gabe pointed to Willy's coffee. "I need it to help me survive this entirely inappropriate conversation."

"My man is honest."

Joy laughed and put her arm around Brian, pulling him close. "Ruthlessly. He never tells a lie. And that's good."

"We know where he stands. Let's get this poor guy some coffee."

"I'm standing right here on Joy's front porch," Brian asserted.

"Right you are, my man. Let's go inside and get your brother's coffee."

They filed into the house, and Joy handed Gabe a big cup of steaming coffee. Lifting his mug in a salute, he said he might survive this conversation after all.

"Do you want to cut it in here?" Brian was ready to cut Willy's hair.

"My hair?" Willy put his hands on his head, and Brian nodded.

"And then again, I might not," Gabe added.

"Sure, why not? Then I wouldn't have to fool with it, right? Get the scissors, Joy." Willy put a barstool in the center of the kitchen and sat, waiting.

Joy went to her bedroom and came out with a pair. "You sure?" she questioned.

Willy closed his eyes, and she snipped, one . . . two . . . He opened them and looked down. "Oh, my hair, my beautiful hair. Delilah, you are cutting away my strength. Don't poke my eyes out." Brian giggled.

"The Philistines did that," Joy proclaimed, interrupting the act. "Now hush. Do you want it cut or not?"

Noticing Brian's giggles, Willy ramped up his act. Each time a dreadlock fell, he threw his hands on his head and cried, "No, Delilah, no. My strength, my great strength." This went on with each snip, and Brian fell on the floor, laughing and rolling around.

Joy was alarmed. "Is he having a seizure?"

But Gabe was grinning. "You might as well finish it. Can't stop now," he commented with a shrug. So she continued to snip the locks off, one by one.

"That's much better," Brian announced.

"Let me run to the cottage and get my razor." Gabe came back and handed it to Joy, but she indicated he should do it. He finished the job, buzzing off the straggling remains. Joy went to her bedroom and returned with a hand mirror.

Willy looked at himself. "It's not too bad. And it will grow, right?"

"You look like a man. I'm going to call you William now," Joy decided.

"You might change my whole life, my man. You don't know what folks have called me. One guy calls me—"

"Don't say it! Little pitchers have big ears." Joy nodded to Brian.

41

Willy—William—looked confused. Gabe, familiar with the expression, said, "Ruthlessly honest, *and* he repeats everything you say. I agree with him, though—it looks nice." He handed him a ball cap. "You might want this, to keep the sun off your head."

"Okay, but Special Forces? I'd never pass. You were SF, dude?" Gabe nodded. "Cool. I've met a real hero."

Gabe shrugged and reached for another cup of coffee. "Now that our adventure is over, how about breakfast? Brian says I make a good breakfast."

Joy handed Gabe eggs and bacon and reached for a loaf of bread. "I thought he was having a seizure, and you were grinning. What was that all about?"

"Brian used to laugh like that when Mom was alive. I never thought he'd get that back. Your friend William is a treasure."

"He is. After we eat, can you help him get his drums in? They're in the van." After another one of Gabe's good breakfasts, that's what they did. And Brian opted to stay in the basement, watching William play.

Gabe and Joy went back to the kitchen to clean up. "Brian doesn't stay with anyone other than me."

"You never get a break?"

"Well, he stays with the psychologist. Sometimes he keeps Brian in his office coloring if I need to get things done, like go to the Social Security office and what not."

They worked side by side. She told him about each member of the band, and he talked about the past few months and Brian's healing from his trauma. William came upstairs. "Your brother has good rhythm."

Gabe acknowledged him with a smile. "Yeah, he does. Like our dad. Where is he?"

"He's downstairs, playing the drums."

Gabe listened. He walked to the top of the stairs and did not hear a thing. He frowned. "I don't hear him."

"Welcome to the twenty-first century, dude." William filled his cup and waved Gabe downstairs. Brian sat in front of the drums, playing with headphones on. "Kids can hear perfectly, and parents don't have to go nuts." He lifted the headphones off. "Keep on playing, my man. Let your brother hear."

"He's really good," Brian informed Gabe. "Show him, William."

Gabe thought every time he heard "William," his new friend got taller. Of course, William did not play with the headphones on, and he moved around those drums with precision while Brian patted his leg in perfect rhythm. "In a couple of years, we'll have him playing in the band." William nodded to the boy.

"Thanks, William."

"You're welcome, Gabe. My pleasure. The kid's a gift in so many ways."

"Yeah, if you have eyes to see it, he is."

"And ears to hear it."

"That, too."

"So, when do I get to see your wings?"

"Joy says you have to have eyes of innocence."

"I lost my innocence years ago—the year my mother died. You wanna play some more, Brian?" He agreed, and William asked if he minded if they went upstairs. "I need to talk to Joy." William patted Brian's shoulder and pointed to himself, indicating he was going upstairs.

"Do you need privacy, or may I join you?" Gabe asked.

"Come on. He seems content."

William sat at the table. "I thought you made cookies, Joy?" Gabe informed him she had given them to Brian and that he was trying not to eat them. "She's a good cook. She fixed us the best meal I've had in ages."

Joy chuckled. "Hot dogs and canned spaghetti are not much competition."

Wringing out the dishtowel, Joy sat. "What's up, William?"

"Bad news. Rocky broke his hand. He won't be playing for at least eight weeks. Maybe never again." He explained the guitarist had been playing backyard football and fell on it when he was tackled. "I never put my hands at risk, but he's young."

"But he knows my style. We can wait."

"He says we need to move on another release—strike while your iron is hot."

"You need to bring this guy Rocky on as your producer, Joy," Gabe suggested.

"Brilliant suggestion! Let's do that, Joy," William agreed.

"It won't be the same."

"No, but he can direct," Gabe pointed out.

"What did you major in, Gabe?" William wanted to know.

"International studies and business."

A tear trickled down Joy's cheek. "I depend on Rocky so much. He gets me."

William took her hand. "It is what it is, Joy. We can't do anything about it."

Brian had come upstairs, and, seeing Joy's tears, he said, "We can pray, Joy. Always."

"Yes, we can, and we will. Will you pray for Rocky, Brian? He plays the guitar, but he hurt his hand."

"Okay. Lord Jesus, make Rocky better—better than ever." He

looked over at Gabe.

"Very appropriate, Bri."

The boy beamed. "I did okay?"

"More than okay, buddy." The boy stood beside Gabe, who put his arm around him.

"Gabe told me to be appropriate, so Joy would want us to be caretakers, William."

"I don't think she'd run you off if you stole the silver."

"William, we never steal! Jesus says we can't steal." The boy looked at Gabe again.

"That's right, Bri. It's in the Ten Commandments."

"And no other gods."

"Right again, smart guy."

"I know you won't steal anything, Brian. What Willy is trying to say is that I'd never want you and Gabe to leave the farm," Joy reassured him.

"His name is *William* now," Brian reminded her. "He looks like a man. He cut those dreadful locks off." Everyone laughed, and Gabe asked Joy if she wanted him to do anything.

"I didn't put my garden maintenance on the caretaker's duties, but the aphids are getting bad on the roses. Would you mind?"

"I'll get right on it."

"Don't stand on the roses, Gabe."

"I won't. I'll put powder on them. I mean, powder you can't eat. It's poison."

"It won't kill the roses?"

"Nope. Only the bad bugs."

CHAPTER 6

The Band Trickles In

JOY SAID STAN would arrive on Thursday, and when he did, Brian wanted to meet him. Stan showed him his instruments, the banjo and the mandolin. He was not fun like William, but Brian tolerated him well. It helped that Joy introduced them and told the boy he would love to hear Stan play the banjo. Brian shrugged, in a very Gabe-like move, making Joy realize how much influence the older brother had on the boy.

Gabe and Brian did not stay at the house long. Before leaving, Gabe gave his report on their activities for the day, which included building a deck on the cottage so he could monitor the comings and goings better.

After the brothers left, Joy explained to Stan that Brian was shy, and William explained that he was a sensitive kid, telling Stan about the parents' accident. Stan was appropriately sympathetic, and he told them Dave would be coming in with a substitute guitarist. Joy still needed to get the new beds, so she and William took the van to load them. She texted Gabe, and William teased her about reporting in to her handyman as they got in the van.

They returned with the beds, and Gabe stepped down from the

developing deck when he heard them, Brian trailing behind. Joy asked Brian to carry the pillows, and Gabe and Stan carried the beds in and up the stairs. Stan watched Gabe go to the linen closet and make up the beds, with Brian's unhelpful, but oh-so-eager assistance. When they went downstairs, Joy invited everyone for lunch, but Brian demurred.

"Joy made the sandwiches—enough for all of us. I see a peanut butter and jelly. Who is that for?" Stan urged the brothers. "Please stay. I want to get to know the guy who got Willy to cut his hair. He looks so good without his dreadful locks. Aren't you responsible for that, Brian?"

Brian grinned and said, "Okay."

"How's the deck coming, Gabe?" Joy asked.

"It's a lot smaller than your deck." Gabe tucked a napkin into Brian's collar and took the chair beside him. "You want to say the blessing, Bri?"

"Would Dad's blessing be appropriate?" At Gabe's nod, he repeated, "Bless us, O Lord, and these thy gifts which we are about to receive. And bless Joy."

"Amen," they echoed. Gabe winked at his brother.

"Did you build the deck behind my bedroom, too?" Joy wondered.

"Dad and I did when I was on leave several years ago."

"It's nice."

"Dad smoked, and Mom didn't want it in the house around Brian. It was a vice we tolerated because . . ." He shrugged.

"Dad loved me, but he didn't know what to do," Brian chimed in. Joy saw Gabe raise his eyebrows. She, too, was surprised at Brian's perceptiveness. "Sometimes I'm difficult. Isn't that right, Gabe?"

"Only sometimes. But most of the time you're special, buddy."

"I think you're cool, my man."

"If you can get this guy to cut off his dreadful locks, you're okay in my book." Stan waved his hand in William's direction.

"They were awful! They stuck up all over his head, and they were dirty! Little bits of stuff stuck in it." Gabe raised his eyebrows, and Brian apologized for not being appropriate, adding, "But they were."

Gabe rolled his eyes, and Joy touched his hand. "Ruthless," she said, in jest.

"Always," Gabe confirmed. And everyone laughed. "Ready to get back to work, kiddo?" Gabe rose and gently removed Brian's napkin. The two of them excused themselves.

"Thank you for the lunch, Joy."

Gabe touched the boy's shoulder. "Very appropriate, buddy. Thanks, Joy."

As they walked off, those around the table heard Brian add, "I guess I showed you, huh?"

Gabe chuckled. "Yes, you did. You reminded me of my manners."

"Isn't that kid a trip?" William picked up his plate.

"He's a neat little kid." Stan also took his to the sink. "Thanks, Joy. I see why you love him. He sure loves you."

"Oh, man, I called her a nag, and he informed me in no uncertain terms she is *not* a nag."

"I need *someone* to stick up for me. So, what do you know about this guitar player, Stan?"

"He's good, but he knows it."

"I told him to listen to all my songs."

"Why don't you come down, and we'll run through your new

one? Why did you give Gabe all the cookies?"

"For Brian."

"Whatever, girl. I'm not a white gal, but even I perceive Gabe is a stud." Joy blushed, and William knew he had hit the nail on the head.

* * *

The next day, when Dave and the new guy, Dean, rolled up in Dave's truck, Joy picked up Stan's meaning within ten minutes. Gabe and Brian had come in to see if she needed anything, when she asked Dean if he had listened to her songs yet.

"Oh, everyone knows your songs. I didn't need to listen."

"I wanted you to hear Rocky. He made some comments as we practiced." Joy marched out of the room and then returned with a stack of her CDs, handing them to him. "We won't start until after you've listened to them." When Dean didn't reach for them, she added, "I mean that. Rocky gets me. Listen to him." Dean enumerated the bands he had accompanied, but she insisted.

"You're holding us up, Joy." With an edge to his voice, Dean added, "I'll get you."

"That's not appropriate."

Dean looked at Brian. "What did you say?"

"That's not appropriate to say to Joy. She's your boss."

"Mouthy little kid, aren't you?"

Joy's jaw dropped, but it was Gabe who responded. "He's honest. Ruthlessly honest. Come on, Bri." Gabe put his arm around his brother and led him to the door.

"Holy cow, Dean, the kid has Down's. I told you that," William reminded him.

Dave looked over at Joy. "I'm sorry, Joy."

49

"*He's* the one you should be sorry to. Now go, listen. Listen to every one of them. You can hear Rocky's comments."

Joy walked over to Gabe's deck and watched him wait for Brian to hand him nails, one by one. Neither of them spoke to or looked at her. "I'm sorry, Gabe."

"Not your problem. I'll keep him with me."

"William loves him."

"But Dean . . . doesn't."

Brian studied his shoes and did not see Joy wipe her eyes. And Gabe did not look up when she left. When she returned to the kitchen, Stan and Dave were doing the dishes. She sat and put her head on her hands.

"No luck?"

"He's going to keep Brian away."

"I get where Gabe is coming from, Joy." William took her hand. "He's protecting him."

"But you and I and Stan will be poorer for it. And I wanted him to help me with a song."

"Dean may wash out sooner than we think, Joy. Especially at the rate he's going. I'm sorry I didn't check him out more closely."

"Not your bad, Dave." Joy cursed softly, and William raised his eyebrows. "It's Rocky's fault, for playing that stupid football game."

Dean returned and said, "I listened to the songs. Every fricking last one of them. I can do this."

After a frustrating afternoon, Joy called Rocky and asked him if he would produce for her, at least until he could come back as her guitarist. She sent him a ticket to fly, and he said he would be there on the next flight. She explained that it was hard to work with Dean.

"I heard he's a prima donna."

"He's an arrogant prima donna, and he insulted my best friend, a kid with Down's. Can you believe that? A sweet, innocent little boy."

"The guys told me about him. Willy says the kid's a kick."

"Brian says he's William now because he got him to cut off his 'dreadful' locks and now he looks like a man."

"This I gotta see! I'll text you the arrival time."

Joy sent Gabe a text, telling him Rocky was coming in the next day to produce, and asking if she and William could come by the cottage that afternoon. She held her breath until he texted back in agreement. With a smiley face, he added that Brian wanted them to come.

Brian ran to William and threw his arms around him.

"I've missed you, my man. What have you been up to?" Brian showed him the deck, telling him he handed Gabe the nails.

"One by one," Joy added.

"You're a big helper, my man. Makes the work go much faster, eh, Gabe?"

"I tried to get him to let me keep a few in my mouth, but he said it might break my teeth."

"So right, Brian. We can't have Gabe lose his teeth." William grinned at Gabe, who rolled his eyes.

"Can I have a hug, Brian?" Joy stretched out her arms, and Brian put his around her, leaning on her breast. She pulled him onto her lap and stroked him on his back. "Thanks for letting us come see you."

"I don't like that Dean guy."

"I don't either. He's not in my band. He's a substitute because my guitarist broke his hand."

"That's good."

"I love you, Brian."

"I love you, too. To the moon and back."

* * *

The next afternoon, Stan drove Joy's Jeep to the airport after she set the GPS for him. She got a text from Gabe: "You gone?"

She texted back: "No. Stan went to get Rocky at the airport."

"Brian wants to come see you. Will you go to the deck?"

"I'll meet him there." She poured three glasses of lemonade and invited Dean to join them in a few minutes. She had a long talk with him the night before, after Brian told her he did not like him, and the other guys joined her in telling him how badly he had treated the boy. He seemed to show some remorse.

Joy was happy to see Brian, and she sang him some of the lyrics to "his" song.

"That's pretty, Joy."

"That's your song, Brian. I'm going to dedicate it to you." She explained to him what that meant, and he was thrilled; his name would be on her album cover. But his face fell when Dean came.

The guitarist told Brian he was sorry and said he wanted to make it up to him. "Joy told me you showed her the stream. Will you show me?"

Brian looked at Joy, and she nodded. "Okay." Brian was reluctant, but Joy knew he wanted to please her. "It's a long walk."

"I can take Dave's truck. We can drive."

"Only to the stream and back."

"Okay, little man."

Gabe rounded the corner about a half an hour later. "Where's

Brian?"

"He went with Dean to show him the stream."

"You let him go?"

"Dean feels bad. We all ganged up on him last night and told him how mean he was to Brian."

"You didn't ask me! You had no right to let him go without asking me." A muscle ticked in Gabe's right cheek. "He's mean, Joy. I've known men like him. I'm going after them." Gabe took off, running.

Gabe was a half a mile down the road when he saw the boy trudging toward him. Dropping to his knees, Gabe held out his arms. Brian threw himself into them, and his big brother drew him into an embrace. "Where is Dean, Bri?"

"We were playing hide-and-seek, and I couldn't find him. I looked and called and called. But I walked to the sun, just like you taught me. It's afternoon, isn't it?"

"Yep. You did the right thing, buddy. Come on, hop on my back and I'll let you ride piggyback." They had only gone ten or fifteen feet when Gabe stopped. "Wait a minute. I need to check this out." Slipping Brian off his back, he leaned to study something on the ground. Quickly gathering the lad up again, he jogged back to Joy's house.

Gabe banged on the door, and Joy answered. "I've gotta go get the . . ." He paused and swore. "Dean left Brian while they were playing hide-and-seek. You stay here with Joy, buddy, and don't leave the house." He looked at her. "Can I trust you to keep him inside?"

"Yes, Gabe. I will. I'm sorry."

Joy watched Stan pull up with Rocky. "What's up? Gabe's got a fire under his butt. He wouldn't even stop to meet Rocky.

53

He ran over to his truck, put a rifle in it, and took off."

Joy paled. "Oh, God. He's furious with Dean, and he's a sniper." Brian stood beside her on the porch. "Let's go inside, Brian. I promised Gabe I'd keep you inside."

"Gabe's mad, Joy. But he won't shoot Dean." They heard a shot. Then another. "He won't, Joy."

After a few minutes, Gabe careened down the road. "Dean is hurt. He tangled with a mama bear. I've got to take him to the hospital. You want to come with me, buddy? It may be a long wait."

"I'll come, too." Joy climbed into the truck beside Gabe, with Brian in the middle.

"Don't let him see the blood, Joy."

They pulled up to the emergency room. Joy had sent information ahead, but she could not see much of what was going on in the back seat because she had to keep Brian diverted from looking. The Emergency Medical Technicians (EMTs) met them outside with a gurney. Joy explained she needed to give them insurance information, and she hopped out. Gabe waited with Brian in the truck. He would have to clean the blood up later. Joy rejoined them after a few minutes. "He'll be okay, but he'll need lots of stitches, and he'll be in at least overnight."

"We need to find the cub," Gabe mentioned on the way home.

"She had a baby?"

"She had milk. That's why she was so vicious."

"Do you think it's big enough to survive?"

"Maybe, maybe not. She was pretty full." They passed the house, continuing up the road. "Stay in the car. Bears don't usually pair, but I don't want you to encounter the dad." Gabe reached for his rifle and got out. Soon, he opened the door again, handing

Joy two tiny cubs. "One more is still alive out there. The runt looks like . . ." He shook his head and left, returning without the third cub. By now, Joy was crooning to the little bears. "Triplets are rare among bears. He was too small. We'll get a bottle at the house. Brian and I fed a baby raccoon a few months ago. He still comes around, doesn't he, Bri?"

"Yeah, for visits."

They pulled up to the house, and the band members rushed out, asking where Dean was and whether he would be okay. They discussed his condition, and William took his little man into his arms. "So, how is the hero of the day?"

"My brother is the hero. He's a soldier."

Joy handed the cubs around, announcing she would warm some milk. Gabe advised watered down canned milk, if she had any.

"It certainly is exciting around here. Makes Nashville seem boring," Rocky said while fighting one of the little bears pulling at his cast bandage. Stan took the cub, and William held the other one.

"I need to get another bottle," Gabe realized.

"The Wildlife guy gave us an extra one, Gabe."

"He sure did, buddy. Let me go look for it. Look at that big guy gobble it up!"

The cubs were hungry. Their mama must have been gone a while, and now she was dead. Joy could tell Gabe hated that. "I need to call the Department of Natural Resources and tell them we have more orphans." He called and explained their situation, and then he hung up. "They said we did so well with Coonie that they trust us to keep the cubs until they can get here. They'll be out in a few days."

"Coonie?" Dave raised his eyebrows.

"Brian named him," Gabe explained. "What shall we call these guys, Bri?"

"Flopsy, and Cottontail?" Brian suggested.

"Works for me." Gabe shrugged. "The big one should be Cottontail. He was always in trouble, getting into Mr. McGregor's garden. Flopsy was a good bunny."

"Can we order pizza?"

"I have some in the freezer, Brian." Joy fetched three out of the refrigerator's freezer, putting two in the oven and setting the third on the counter.

Dave ran up the stairs, bringing back a six pack of sodas. "Willy—William—said you didn't have any, so we brought some."

Gabe reached for a glass and put ice in it. Brian reminded him he does not drink Cokes. "Tonight, I do, buddy. You want some, too?"

Brian tilted his head. "No, I'm healthy. I'll drink milk."

"Good choice, Bri. Now make another good one and blow on the pizza before you take a bite."

"I didn't do that last time. I burned my mouth."

Joy lifted out two steaming pizzas and put the third one in. Then she went to the phone and called the hospital. "He's resting," she reported. "They have him sedated. I hate that no one is with him."

"I hate that he left Brian. Thank God Brian left before the mama bear got there."

"I'm so sorry, Gabe. I never expected him to do that."

Gabe kept his head down. "Bullies never change, Joy. You're a good person. You wouldn't know that."

"Next time, I'll ask."

Stan explained, "She thinks you'll never leave Brian with her again."

"I've never left him with anyone, except the psychologist." Gabe looked up. "Thanks, Joy. I know you wouldn't hurt him."

CHAPTER 7

Who Is Playing That Guitar?

AFTER THEY FINISHED the pizzas and cleaned up, Gabe took Brian home. On the way to the cottage, Gabe said, "I probably stink, and maybe you do, too. Let's get a shower." As usual, Brian sat on the commode with the lid down while Gabe showered. "Your turn, buddy."

Gabe trimmed his hair while his brother showered, and when Brian got out, he asked if Gabe would play the guitar for him. "Some of Mama's favorites."

"Okay, buddy." His brother had a rough day, and he would do whatever it took to get his mind off the incident with Dean.

Brian insisted on sitting on the new deck, so Gabe set a couple of chairs there, side by side. He loved to watch the boy's face light up when he played, which always set the boy's foot to tapping. Brian only recently began to ask him to play their mama's favorites, and Gabe remembered many happy evenings with his mom singing along. Her voice was not as beautiful as Joy's, but it was pleasant. Brian must have gotten his rhythm from their dad, because Dad used to tap his toe, too.

"Hi, guys, what's up? Do you need anything?" Gabe stopped playing. He had been rapping out percussion on the side of his guitar and picking out the tune, not simply strumming. "We heard you play whatever Brian asks." Joy's hands slammed on her hips as she stared at him. "Gabe, we need *you* in the band. You've been hiding your light under a bushel."

Gabe shrugged. "I kick it around a little."

Brian took Joy's hand. "I told you he plays the guitar."

"You did, Brian. I didn't know how well he plays, though."

"Gabe does everything good. He shoots good. He hunts good. He fishes good. He builds good, too. But he don't—doesn't—cook so good. Not as good as you."

"I used to play for Mom a lot, and at the camp, sometimes at USO." Gabe shrugged.

"I'm never listening to that shrug again!"

"How can you listen to a shrug, Joy?"

William, who had also joined them, shook his head and laughed. Brian stared at Joy with a questioning look on his face, waiting for her to answer him. "Oh, your brother shrugs eloquently, Brian."

"What does that mean, Gabe?"

"Not sure, buddy."

"We were on the porch when heard you, Gabe," Rocky explained as he, Stan, and Dave now approached them. "You're good, so I called Joy to come listen and asked her who it was. We figured it had to be you, and William and Stan wanted to see for themselves. You're the answer to Joy's prayers."

"Joy said it sounded live," Stan added.

"And I told the guys that, along with his wings, Gabe plays the guitar," William finished.

"Wings?" Dave parroted.

"Yep. But I haven't seen them yet." William winked at Stan.

59

Rocky added on with, "I said, 'Whoever he is, he's terrific!' I noticed you even got the percussion in there."

"I'm no performer," Gabe shrugged.

Joy put her hands over her eyes. "Not seeing that shrug, Gabe. Not listening to it, not seeing it. You're a performer now."

"But I have to take care of Brian."

"You'll be our mascot, won't you, my man?"

"What's a mascot?"

Stan explained it to him, but the boy replied, "Not tomorrow. I want to see Dean."

"But he left you, Bri." Gabe shook his head.

"He got hurt. We should go see him."

Gabe stiffened and heaved a sigh. "Okay, we'll go see him. Brian wakes up about eight. We'll check in at the hospital and be back by ten."

"You've got your guitarist, Joy." Rocky led the way across the driveway as they talked.

"Right under my nose. And he says he 'kicks it around a little.' The man's got serious talent!"

Rocky agreed, adding, "He has talent, and you two will sync nicely."

* * *

Gabe called the hospital the next morning, learning Dean would remain there at least another day. He was on IV antibiotics to prevent infection, and pain medication. After ascertaining the boy truly did want to go, Gabe drove Brian to the hospital. He led his brother through the halls and pushed open the door.

Dean winced, averting his eyes. "Did you come to finish the job, Gabe?"

"I figure you learned your lesson. But I'd like to know why you thought it was fun to hide from a little kid?"

"At first it was kinda funny, listening to him looking for me. But then it got quiet, and I came out and couldn't find him. Then I heard the bear. She was plenty mad, and she jumped me."

"You must have been in the cave. She had cubs behind you."

"I got hurt—mostly on my back. Doc says I'll play again, but it will be a while."

"Gabe's gonna play with the band." Brian looked up at his brother. "Aren't you, Gabe?"

"Are you that good?"

"I'm all they've got, Dean. As for you, you're leaving as soon as you are able."

"I figured you'd say that. Plus, Joy has the hots for you. So it's a done deal."

Gabe approached the bed, his fists clenched. The muscle in his right cheek ticked. "You'd better not say that again, or I *will* finish the job. Ask the doctor when you can leave, and I'll fly you back if I have to pay for it myself."

"You won't have to. Miss Bluegrass Nashville will pay for it. I heard her homeowners insurance is paying for my hospitalization. If I'd lost the use of my hands, I'd sue her. Maybe I still will, if my back is messed up for good."

Gabe's eyes narrowed. "So, you abandon a kid with Down's, I save your life with a sniper shot—it took two, one to get her to look up and one to take her out—and you're going to sue Joy? I should have left you to die!"

Brian looked from one man to the other. "You wouldn't let him die, Gabe."

"Maybe, maybe not. It would be a hard choice, Bri. We need

61

to leave now, before I do something stupid." He took his brother's hand and led him out the door. As usual, he was gentle with Brian as he buckled him in. He had spent half an hour earlier getting the blood off the back seat. And he did not say a word as they drove back to the house.

"Are you mad, Gabe? Did I do something not appropriate?"

"You were fine. I'm not mad at you. I'm mad at Dean. I needed to get out of there before I punched a man in a hospital bed. If he hadn't played his silly games, none of this would have happened. The only thing inappropriate is that you don't need to feel bad when someone does bad things to you. And don't *ever* leave again without telling me, okay?"

"Yes, sir."

"Hey! You make me feel as old as Dad."

"I'm glad you're going to play in the band."

"I'm scared about that. I'm no musician."

"You play the guitar good, Gabe."

"You are prejudging, buddy. Joy's band members are all professionals."

"What's a judge, like you said?" Gabe tried his best to explain it, but Brian told him the other band members thought he was good, too.

They turned into the long driveway and saw someone looking down the road. They pulled up in front of their parents' old home, and William broke into a grin. "Rocky is already putting us through our paces. That was a great idea, Gabe. He's going to be a good on-site producer."

"Yeah, but he doesn't have much to work with in me. I'm no professional."

"He was her guitarist; he knows what she likes. You want

something to eat?"

Brian wanted cereal again, and Gabe grabbed an apple. "*There* you are," Joy said, coming into the kitchen. "How did the visit go?"

"I barely kept from punching a guy in a hospital bed. That's all I'll say."

She looked at Brian. "Gabe didn't want him to sue you, Joy."

"Sue me? Gabe saved his life. You'd think he'd be grateful."

"Not so much. As soon as the doctor lets him out, I want him on the first plane out of here."

"He will be, Gabe." Joy placed her hand on his muscled forearm. "Are you ready to play? You can use Dean's guitar today, but Rocky is having his mom overnight his for you."

"Look, Joy, you don't have to do this. I'm no professional."

"Methinks thou dost underestimate thyself. Rocky is a terrific producer, by the way. He's rearranging everything we've been doing the last few days." She waved him down the basement stairs while holding Brian's hand.

Gabe ran through a few of their songs on the guitar, studying Joy's face each time he stumbled. "I don't read music. I play by ear. Some of these I've never heard before."

"Those are the new ones. You're doing okay, and we'll have you reading music before long," Dave said. "I know you were in Special Forces—Willy showed me the hat. How many languages do you speak?"

"Arabic and Farsi, pretty well. Kurdish is tolerable—I understand a lot, but can't speak it well."

"Music is just another language, and not nearly as tough as those." Stan chuckled. "You'll get it."

Rocky handed Gabe the CDs Joy had previously given Dean.

"You should listen to these."

"Thanks, man. I'll get right on it."

Joy had gone up to fix lunch, taking Brian with her. She called down to them, and they trooped up. When Gabe got to the top of the stairs, he watched Joy and Brian from the doorway, grateful to her for including the lad in what she was doing.

"Okay, Brian, put the chips on the table and I'll set out the sandwiches. Can you put the plates around for everybody? We have William, Dave, Stan, Rocky, Gabe, and me. How many does that make?"

Reciting softly, Brian counted on his fingers. "Six. And me, that makes seven. And we need napkins, too."

"Right you are!" She counted them out and handed them to him.

Brian folded the napkins in half and put one beside each plate. "Gabe prays good, too."

"I won't ever underestimate him again. Gabe, would you pray?" They all bowed their heads and then passed the sandwiches around.

Brian looked up at Gabe and announced, "She made tuna fish for you and peanut butter for me."

"Um, could you give him some jelly? He really likes jelly, don't you, buddy?"

"I found some in the cabinet." She handed it to him.

"My favorite—Mama's jelly. Can you make jelly, Joy? Does she have a recipe?"

Gabe shrugged.

"You can look it up on the net," Stan suggested.

"But Mama's is special. Dad said so."

Noting the impending waterworks, Gabe picked up a knife.

"Can you tuck your napkin in while I spread this good jelly?" Brian gave it his best attempt, and Gabe straightened it, giving the boy a little pat on his chest. "There, is that good?"

Brian grinned through his jelly-smeared lips. "Yep. Good."

"Would it disturb anyone if I let him listen to my iPad?"

"We've got headphones. Remember, big brother?" William reminded him.

"Can I play the drums, William?"

"Maybe after a bit, my man. We have to get back to work." Brian looked disconsolate, but Gabe assured him William would let him play drums later. For now, they needed him to help Joy sing.

"Okay."

When they got back downstairs, Dave and Stan moved a chair near to where they practiced. Gabe found a YouTube channel about heavy equipment for Brian to watch. They heard him giggle, and once he even laughed out loud.

Gabe glanced over at him. "Sometimes third-world drivers mess up on there. He gets a kick out of that." William went to look over Brian's shoulder and started laughing himself.

"While they are doing that, let me show you a few things, Gabe." Rocky gave him a brief lesson, pointing out whole notes, half notes, and rests.

The guys came back over, and William was wiping his eyes. "That's the funniest thing I ever saw!" Seeing Gabe getting frustrated, Rocky suggested playing some of Joy's familiar songs. Things went smoothly after that, and Gabe relaxed, especially when Joy praised him.

"Rocky gave you the singles to listen to?" she asked.

"He did, and I'll start tonight." Gabe glanced down at his

hands.

"They're tender?" Rocky assumed. "We're used to playing all day, but maybe you need a break."

"Sorry," Gabe apologized.

"Hey, my man, can I watch?" William reached for the iPad.

"It quit."

"Probably needs a charge. I'll run get my charger." Dave ran up the stairs.

"We need to feed the cubs anyway," Joy remembered. The wildlife folks called this morning, and they're coming tomorrow. I forgot to tell you, Gabe."

Stretching his hands, Gabe said he hated saddling the band with the cubs, but he could not let the poor things die after he killed their mama. He asked Brian if he wanted to take a walk with him and listen to Joy's songs.

"Okay." The boy slipped his hand into Gabe's.

Dave ran after them with an MP3 player on a leather string. "Here, you can use this. Want earphones?"

"We both want to listen. Don't we, Bri?" Gabe hung it around his neck. "Thanks, Dave."

CHAPTER 8

Getting Lovers Together

JOY WENT OUT onto the front porch to watch Gabe and Brian as they walked down the road together. Gabe was tall but slender. *Wasn't he a quarterback in high school?* Unlike most men who left high school football behind, he was trim and more muscular due to his time in Special Forces. On their bike ride, he had hung back for her and Brian. He told her he missed long-distance running and biking. His life revolved around his brother now. She could not believe he never left the boy with anyone. He was quite a guy. She sighed, thinking it was too bad she blew it.

William stepped outside and dropped into a chair beside her. Seeing her watching the brothers, he teased, "Doing a little day-dreaming about your stud-man, girl?"

She burst into tears.

"What is it?" William put his arm around her.

"I blew it, William. He hates me now!"

"What? He does not!"

"He does. I sent his precious little buddy with that vile man." She wiped her eyes. "Dean could have gotten him killed."

"Baby, that man Gabe is stuck on you like that stuff they put boats together with after they saw them in half. Come on, where

67

did you come up with that idea?"

"When I went over to apologize, he wouldn't even look at me. He kept his head down and kept pounding nails."

"But he couldn't keep his eyes off you today. And whenever you praised him, he stood so tall and proud I thought he was going to snap off a salute. Tell me what it means when a guy has 'the hots' for you?"

"Who said that?"

"Dean did, about Gabe. Then Brian asked me what that meant, because Gabe got so mad when he said it. Dean sees it. I see it. The guys see it. Come on, Joy."

"What did you tell Brian?"

"I told him it meant Gabe wants to marry you—left the graphic stuff off."

She sniffed. "If he has the hots for me, he has a funny way of showing it."

"Brian also said Gabe told him you are his boss, and it wasn't appropriate."

"I don't want to be his *boss*, William. I want to be his . . . his—"

"But Gabe didn't deny it. He's out there studying your songs so he can play them. What's a fellow got to do to show you he loves you, Joy?"

"Maybe . . . maybe kiss me?"

William sat, slapping his hands on his knees and laughing. Dave came out to join them. "What's up, Joy?"

"She thinks Gabe hates her."

"That's nuts. He's crazy about you!"

"I *told* you, girl. Let's get everybody out here and take a vote."

"Stop it, William. I'm humiliated enough."

"Tell you what," Dave suggested, "we've got the night off. You fix him a nice dinner, and we'll all leave. We'll get out of here—leave you alone. The two of you."

"The three of us, you mean," she corrected him. "And Gabe certainly wouldn't do anything that isn't 'appropriate' in front of his little brother."

"Oh, so you want him to do something inappropriate, hmm?" Dave winked at William.

"Yes! Yes, I do."

"We need to rethink this. How can we get two people who love each other to . . . to . . ."

Joy ran into the house and locked herself in her bedroom. Dave listened at the door, and Stan went over and asked what was going on.

"She's crying," Dave reported.

"Why?"

"She thinks Gabe hates her," William explained. "I tried to convince her, but . . ." He shook his head. "She wants him to kiss her."

"Stand in line—every male in Nashville wants to kiss her. What's his problem?" Stan looked around.

"She's his boss. Brian told me Gabe said it isn't appropriate."

Dave, Stan, and William went back to the porch to confer. They were sitting there when Brian and Gabe returned.

"Thanks, Dave, this helps a lot. Tomorrow, I'll do better," Gabe said with confidence.

"You're doing great, Gabe. You can't integrate into a band in half a day. Good grief, the two of you are nuts. Gabe doesn't think he can play, and Joy is in her room crying her head off."

"Joy is crying? Why?"

"Because she thinks you hate her. She won't open the door. Maybe you'd better go check."

As Gabe went into the house, William snagged Brian before he could follow, whispering, "We need to leave them alone to work this out. He loves her, and she loves him. But they need to figure it out. Let's leave them alone, okay?"

Brian put his hand over his mouth. His eyes were wide, and he threw his arms around William's neck. "Really?" he whispered.

"Without a doubt. She told me."

"But Gabe told me it wasn't appropriate."

"She can change his mind about that."

"She can? So, he can have the hots for her?"

The guys cracked up. "I told the kid having the hots for someone means you want to marry them," William said defensively.

"In the proper order, I guess it does. This is a Christian band." And Dave guffawed.

"What's so funny?" Brian inquired.

Stan dropped a hand on his shoulder. "Don't believe everything this guy tells you. Those earphones are waiting for you downstairs. Want to play the drums?"

"Oh, yeah. Can I?"

CHAPTER 9

Joy Is Convinced

GABE HEARD HER CRYING, and it tore his heart out. "Joy, it's Gabe. May I come in?"

"No!"

"Why are you crying? Did someone upset you?" The crying continued. "How can I help if you don't tell me what's wrong?"

"*You* are what's wrong. Now go away."

"That's crazy. If I'm what's wrong, and you send me away, how can we resolve this?" The sobs settled to sniffles, and Gabe tried the door. Locked. "Look, I have a set of keys, and I'm coming in."

"I look horrible."

"You couldn't look horrible if you tried." Then quiet. "May I come in now? Please? I listened to all the songs, and I can play them now. But you don't have to do this. You can get a professional."

The door flew open. "You numbskull! I don't want a professional. I want *you*."

"Okay, here I am." He shrugged. "What do we need to resolve?" Tears threatened her face again. "I'll fix it, if I know what to do." Her face flamed. "What? Was one of the guys inappropri-

71

ate? I'll take him down. What happened?" Tears began to trickle. He was undone. He leaned in and kissed each one. Her arms came around his neck, and he kissed her—*really* kissed her. "Don't cry, baby, don't cry."

"I thought you hated me."

"Hate you? Why would I hate you?"

"Be . . . be . . ." She sniffed. "Because I let your buddy go off with that vile man, and he could have been killed."

"But he wasn't. He's fine." Gabe cradled her head in his neck. "He's probably scared silly because he heard you were crying, and he adores you. I adore you. You've brought more joy into our lives in the past weeks than we've known in a long, long time."

"I have?"

"Yep. Brian calls it Joy-joy." He chuckled. "Reminds me of that old song from Bible school, 'I've got that joy, joy, joy, down in my heart.' And that's where you are, baby—down in my heart. Down so deep I'll never let you out. I tried to resist you. I rode away on the bike, but I couldn't escape you."

Joy put her long, slender hands on the sides of his face. He had been jealous of Brian when she put her hands on his face like that. Now she did it to him, and he felt her tenderness, relished her touch. He closed his eyes. He was falling . . . falling . . . *Was this falling in love?* She pressed her soft lips to his, and he was home. Thrusting his fingers into her long blonde hair, he drew her to him and kissed her again. "Maybe this is too soon, but I love you, Joy."

"I loved you by day two."

"We need to go tell Brian. He wanted me to marry you when we were riding our bikes. Remember his 'she loves me, she loves me not?' He wasn't talking about a girlfriend. He was talking

72

about you and me."

"The little romantic!"

"He's never taken to anyone the way he took to you. But you are irresistible, and he has good taste."

When the couple emerged from the bedroom, Gabe looked around and asked where Brian was. Dave told him he was downstairs playing the drums. "I see all's well with you two."

Joy beamed, and her fair cheeks were pinked with whisker burns. "He convinced me."

"I can see," Dave said, observing her face. "Told ya."

"All you had to do was look at the guy—totally besotted," William clapped Gabe on the back.

"She is so precious with Brian, and he adores her."

"And it doesn't hurt that she's gorgeous, Gabe," Stan teased.

"Nope." Gabe put his arm around Joy. "That you are, baby. Let's go tell my brother."

"Uh, if he asks you if you have the hots for her, I told him that means you want to marry her," William explained. "He told me what Dean said and asked me what it meant. Sorry if that rushes you."

Taking Joy's hand, Gabe pulled her to the top of the basement steps. Brian looked up with a question in his eyes and took off the headphones.

"I find it very appropriate that your brother loves me, Brian."

He almost knocked the drums over scrambling up to throw his arms around Joy. "Stan told me I couldn't believe all William said. He told me you love Gabe, and I asked if he has the hots for you."

Gabe could not help but chuckle as he put his arm around his brother. "I do, but that's not the appropriate way to say it. Please drop that phrase."

"It's not appropriate?" Gabe shook his head. "But you're gonna marry her?"

"Yep. If she'll have us."

"Will you have us, Joy? Will you? Please?"

"I can't imagine life without you, Brian. You and Gabe."

"Does that mean yes, Gabe?"

"That means yes, Bri. How did we get so lucky, huh?"

"Yes! I gotta tell the guys." Brian tore up the stairs, finding William, Stan, Dave, and Rocky all waiting for him.

"Aren't you glad you gave them a little time to work this out, my man?"

"She's gonna marry us! Gabe says he has the hots for her, but that's not an appropriate way to say it."

"I agree. Dean said that about Joy to be mean," Stan replied. "It isn't nice."

"She's nice. Why would he be mean to her?"

"The same reason he hid from you, my man. He's a mean guy."

"I wanted to see him because he was hurt, but he and Gabe got angry. He wanted to sue Joy. That's mean, isn't it?"

William's mouth dropped open when he heard that. "He would be dead if Gabe hadn't shot that bear!"

"Speaking of bears, isn't it time to feed the cubs?" This time, it was Dave who remembered.

"I bet Joy was up with them last night. She seemed tired today." Stan went over to the box and picked up the loudest one— Cottontail.

"She thought Gabe hated her. That's why she seemed tired today." William reached for the other one.

Dave had gone to get milk out of the refrigerator and heat it. "I agree—Peter Cottontail is bigger."

CHAPTER 10

Wedding Plans

AFTER SUPPER, SEVERAL of the guys went to a movie, and Gabe and Brian walked home to their cottage with Joy. Brian snuggled between them on the couch on the deck, and Gabe asked about the next step. Now that everything was in the open, he wanted to move forward as quickly as possible, because he did have the hots for this beautiful woman.

"I guess we need to call your parents, although I don't see how I can get over to Nashville. Not with Brian."

"I told my folks about you two. They remember the Winslows very well, although Brian was born after we left." She pulled him close. "I told them how special you are."

"And you love me, right?"

She put her slender hands on the boy's face and brought his eyes up to meet hers in a gesture Gabe had now also experienced. It was Gabe's first realization of their unique relationship. Before this, Brian would not accept intimacy from anyone except his parents and eventually him. And it had taken him months to establish it.

"Yes, I love you very much."

"I love you, and Gabe loves you, and you're going to marry us."

Gabe winked at his brother. He was not jealous of Joy's affection for Brian—it was one of the things that attracted him to her, her tenderness toward this unique child. He did, however, also remember the slender leg emerging from the limo as she sang and walked into his heart.

"Mom and Dad remembered your scholarship to Virginia Tech, and the foster kids your folks took in. They admired your folks a lot. Mom said you were a fine family."

"They were super, huh, Bri?" This time, Gabe gathered the boy into a hug.

"Oh, look!" Joy pointed. "Did you see the falling star?"

"We're supposed to have a meteor shower tonight." Gabe looked at his watch. "It's late, buddy. We need to get you to bed."

"Aw, can't I watch?"

"Maybe for a bit. Come, get on my lap." Gabe pulled his brother onto his lap, knowing he would be out before long. He slipped his arm around Joy, and she snuggled to him, taking Brian's hand. They fell silent, only crying out whenever they saw another meteor. Gabe reached back and pulled a blanket around them. "This is nice."

"How do you say it, Gabe?"

"Cozy?" Gabe looked down at the sleepy boy.

"Yeah. Cozy."

Seeing Brian dozing off, the adults fell silent again, and Gabe carried Brian inside. Once back outside, Gabe and Joy resumed conversation. "Dr. Wells said you've brought Brian a lot of healing, Joy."

"I'm glad."

"He'll be a problem, though." When she asked how so, Gabe told her how his brother sat on the commode when he showered and how he had to remain in the bathroom while Brian took his.

"But when I'm here, I'll read to him or play fish and give you a little privacy. How have you done that 'til now, Gabe? He's your constant shadow."

He leaned back, thinking. "First, I lived in the BOQ a while." He had to explain Bachelor Officers Quarters to her. "But living with Brian wasn't a problem anyway. We were both so devastated by our loss; we kind of clung to one another. The psychologist, Dr. Wells, was a tremendous help—to both of us. Look, did you see that one?"

"It was right over us! Can I have more covers?"

Gabe tucked the blanket and kept his arms around her. Her head rested on his chest, and he twirled one of her golden curls in his hand. She glanced up at him, and he lowered his lips to claim hers. "I feel like I'm finally home, Joy."

"Me, too." She pulled him down for another long and lingering kiss.

"Where can we get married? I can't take Brian to Nashville."

"We'll get married at Quiet Dell. Let's talk to Pastor Davis this week."

"Brian goes to Dr. Wells on Tuesday. I'll call and see if we can have an appointment then. I know this is pretty sudden. Do you want to wait?"

"No."

"Good!"

"Got the hots, do you?" She giggled.

"Oh, baby, if you only knew."

"I do. The feeling is mutual." He groaned. "I remember that groan. You did that after our bike ride."

"Yeah, when you said you had to go soak those legs." She

giggled at Gabe again. "I see the guys getting back. You should walk with them." Gabe stood and offered her his hand.

"You'd better stay, in case he wakes up." Joy called to the guys, letting them know she would be right over. "See you in the morning."

"Rocky gave me some goop to toughen my fingers. We'll be there bright and early."

Lifting his hands to her lips, Joy kissed them. Gabe felt healing in her kisses. "Love you," she whispered.

* * *

The next day flew by. Practice went smooth, Brian was content with his iPad, William set him up with his drums while they ate lunch, and Gabe and Joy called her folks that night. Even though Joy's parents felt it was sudden—her father reminding Gabe marriage is for lifetime—they said they thought highly of Gabe's parents and remembered him as well. Finally, her father suggested a trip to the farm in a few days to discuss it further, and Joy urged him to bring her sisters.

On Tuesday, after Gabe and Joy dropped Brian off at the psychologist, they met with Pastor Davis, and he scheduled some marriage counseling, also reminding them marriage is a lifetime commitment. When they went to pick up Brian, Dr. Wells urged them to come in. He settled the boy in his office with some coloring sheets. Brian was excited they were getting married, and Dr. Wells praised them for including him. "He said you are marrying *them*, Joy. I've been aware of your impact on Brian. He's made significant progress since he told you about his parents' death, and I gather he comes into his old house often now."

"He only came into the bedroom once, and Gabe had rearranged it a lot. But he comes into the kitchen and basement daily. One of the guys lets him play the drums."

"Ah," the psychologist said with a smile. "That would be William with the 'dreadful' locks."

"Oh, I forgot to tell you. He had a laughing fit that day, like the old days when Mom was alive. I never thought I'd see that Brian again, but it was pretty funny." Gabe described how William had egged him on, and he now joined the doctor in a chuckle.

"You realize, Joy, that this little boy never allowed intimacy with anyone except his mother, and with Gabe after several months."

"I don't know why he took to me."

"She's pretty special, Dr. Wells. She draws people into her orbit of love quickly. She's kind of hard to resist. I mean, look at me."

"She's not bad on the eyes either, is she?" The good doctor winked at Gabe, and Joy blushed. "Brian has insight, despite his limitations." He stood, offering Joy his hand and bringing his other one around hers. "Brian is a good child, but he can be . . . difficult, mind you."

"Oh, and another thing . . ." Gabe told the doctor what Brian said about their father—that their dad had loved him—and about Brian's admission that he was "difficult."

"When I explained to him about the band, he asked if I told them he was 'different,'" Joy joined in. "I told him I said he was special and that I love him."

Dr. Wells caught Gabe's eye. "This one's special, too, Gabe. Hang on to her."

Gabe put his arm around Joy and promised he had every intention of doing that.

* * *

Within two days, Joy presented the band with a new song: "Winslow Farm." Gabe surprised them all with another couple stanzas of it the next day. When he sang it to them, Rocky's mouth dropped open. "And the man can *sing*." Gabe shrugged. Rocky put him together with Joy, and the sound was remarkable. "We need to get this out as a single. It'll rocket to the top of the charts!"

The band focused on that song for several days and sent it to their publicist, who wanted it out immediately. He also wanted to run a story when he found out about the impending marriage, but Gabe wanted to take some time to get Joy a ring first. After a bit of an argument, she convinced him she wanted a miniature of his ROTC ring. He special-ordered it, and he received it the day before her parents arrived.

The visit from Joy's parents went well. They stayed in a hotel, but her two sisters slept in the house, bunking with Joy. They met Pastor Davis, saw the church, and even picked out bridesmaid dresses for the girls. Joy had already picked out a dress for herself online.

Mr. Thomas sat with Gabe on the cottage's deck one evening and had a heart-to-heart with him, asking how long his parents had been married. "They'd been married twenty-five years when Brian came. Mom was embarrassed to be pregnant for their anniversary party, and, despite his difficulties, she loved Brian immensely."

"I imagine she did. She did well with those foster kids. I was teaching at Byrd at the time, but I had taught at South Harrison, and my former colleagues there bragged about her influence on those kids. She was a good woman, Gabe, and I'm sorry for your loss."

"I had the world's best parents, and I'm sorry Brian lost them so young."

"I honor your decision to give up your career to raise him."

"I wouldn't trade him for the world."

"I can tell. He's blessed to have you."

"No, sir, I'm blessed to have him. And we're both blessed to have Joy."

"Joy is crazy about him. He's all we hear about when we call—and you, of course." Mr. Thomas handed Gabe his empty Coke can and stood. "Best be off to pick up Martha and head to the hotel. Why don't you call me Hap, son?"

"Yes, sir." Gabe looked down at his phone. "Who is Monte Springer?"

"He's her publicist. Why would he be calling you?"

Gabe shrugged and took the call. He frowned and nodded his head, looking up at Joy's father. "You'd better sit back down." When he terminated the call, Gabe looked serious.

"What's up, Gabe?"

"Monte tells me Joy has a serious stalker, and we need to get her some protection. He suggested a guardhouse with a twenty-four-hour guard. He's sending a check for it, but I'll start right away."

"I guess it comes with the business."

"They brought in a profiler. She gets mail once or twice a day from the guy, and the stuff gets viler every day. He's going to overnight copies for me to read. He remembered she has a care-taker here, so he looked up my number on the contract and called. This is serious stuff, Hap. We need to move up this wedding right away. I'm a sniper, and I want to be with her twenty-four/seven."

"Martha won't like that, but I'll explain it to her. I'll call the office and delay my return."

"Send the guys over here, will you? I need to brief them." When they arrived, they informed Gabe that Hap had asked Brian to show him the drums. *Good man. He picked up quickly and knew what to do.*

"What's up, Gabe?" the eager band members wanted to know. He filled them in, relaying some of the vulgar messages Monte said the man sent, and what the profiler said.

"That's sick!" Rocky expressed his horror. The other guys agreed.

Gabe explained he would begin construction on a guardhouse and hire guards around the clock. "Thing is, we have 120 acres. I'll have to string razor wire around the entire place."

"You can't build it yourself—she'll suspect something funny," Stan pointed out. "You need to keep playing in the band."

"Dear God, we have to stop 'Winslow Farm' from being released!" Dave looked from one face to another.

"Too late. It's already out and moving up the charts. Came out the first of the week." Alarm crossed William's face as he spoke. "He'll know where she is. I'm sure he knows she comes from Lost Creek, West Virginia."

"Pray like you've never prayed before. I've got to get Brian." With that, Gabe was off.

CHAPTER 11

Quick Wedding

HAP SAT HIS wife down in the hotel, telling her what was happening and stressing the emergency. "I know you want a nice dress and all the trimmings, but you looked lovely in that pink dress at the charity ball last week. Did you know Gabe was a sniper? He wants this wedding as quick as possible so he can be with her twenty-four/seven, and I agree."

Recognizing the advantages of that plan, Martha agreed, and they discussed how they would present it to their daughter. Thankfully, they had already selected dresses for her sisters, and Hap called his office the next day to clear his schedule. They went over to the house about ten, noticing Gabe already had men working on the guardhouse but was in the kitchen drinking a cup of coffee.

"The office called me," Hap said after he hugged Joy. "Can you move this deal up, Gabe? I have time off. Seems my trial has been postponed and rescheduled for later this summer."

"I'll call Pastor Davis right away."

"This is a big change, Daddy. You and Gabe must have had a nice talk last night."

"Fine man, Joy. You couldn't find a nicer fellow."

"Where did he go?"

"He went over to the cottage to call Pastor Davis," Stan reported.

"Why didn't he call from here?"

"Who knows why a lusty groom wants to schedule a wedding right away?" Stan winked at the guys. Joy blushed.

Gabe came in. "Pastor's checking on some things."

"Your package came in at eight, Gabe. I've got it upstairs. Follow me." Dave waved him upstairs. "Willy has Brian playing downstairs. By the way, the alarm already works. The deliveryman had to ring to get in. I drove up and got him."

Gabe tore open the package. His face paled as he handed the threats over after reading them.

"This guy is a nutcase, Gabe!"

"Yeah, he's crazy. But worse, he's dangerous. Remember the guy who shot President Reagan?"

"He doesn't want to *shoot* Joy. He wants to—"

"Not on my watch."

"Gabe, he wants to take *you* out. Look at this." Dave handed him a letter from the stack. "He wants a virgin, he says. And he says you'll never get to her first."

"He knows about me?"

"He knows everything about her. Remember the huge bouquet he sent to the Nashville office on her birthday?"

"I've got every retired military guy out here rolling razor wire and building that guardhouse. We'll buckle down. He's only one guy."

"Yeah, one sick guy."

The muscle in Gabe's right cheek ticked. "But a lot of folks who love her."

Dave shoved the stack under the pillow right before Joy walked in the door. "I can't believe this. Daddy had to check you out, and now he's pushing me to get married? What did you guys talk about last night?"

Gabe took her in his arms and kissed her cheek and then briefly on the lips. "My favorite subject: you."

"I get the feeling I'm intruding." With a wink, Dave walked out the door, and Gabe applied himself to making Joy forget her questions. When she seemed thoroughly distracted, he took her hand and suggested they look for Brian, which they did.

Hearing a bell, Gabe looked around. Dave pointed to a box by the door, and Gabe spoke into it. A voice on the other end told him a man who called himself Pastor Davis was at the gate, and it asked whether to let the man in. Gabe asked to speak to the man, and when he recognized the pastor's voice, he cleared him for entry. Joy stood, looking at Gabe and tapping her foot, arms crossed over her bosom.

"What, baby? Wanna get married?"

"What's going on, Gabe?"

Gabe opened the door for the pastor, who looked from one of them to the other. "We have a reluctant bride here, Pastor."

"I'm not reluctant. I just want to know what's going on. In twenty-four hours, my house has turned into a fortress with alarms ringing, packages coming . . . And my father, who urged me to slow down, now wants me married right away."

"What should I tell her, Pastor?"

"She needs to know. Can we go to a quiet place?"

Joy led them into her bedroom, kicking aside the girls' bedrolls. Gabe sat her on the love seat. "Monte called me last night when your dad was down at the cottage, so he already knows this.

It seems the guy who sends you flowers is a serious stalker. Monte suggested we build a guardhouse and monitor it twenty-four/seven. I told him I was a sniper and that I want to get married right away so I can be with you all the time. He agreed."

"Oh, pooh." Joy waved her hand dismissively. "This happens sometimes."

"We can't pooh-pooh this, baby. Monte brought in a profiler, and he says it's for real. He sent copies of the guy's letters—copies I never want you to see. It's scary stuff. The guy is dangerous."

"And he wants to take Gabe out." Pastor Davis knew that would get Joy's attention.

Tears rolled down Joy's cheeks. Gabe wiped them away. Lifting her eyes, she whispered, "Is this real?"

"We can get you married by Friday. I'll swear an affidavit validating your signatures on the license. I have the papers for you to fill out here. You don't need to leave the house." Pastor Davis reached into his breast pocket and handed them over.

Joy buried her face in Gabe's chest, and he stroked her golden curls. "Not the most romantic thing I can think of—but the only thing. I talked to your dad, Joy. I told him about being a sniper and about the bear that attacked Dean. He agreed with me that this is for the best. What happened to the cubs anyway?"

"DNR took them. Thank God that confusion is lifted."

Hearing Brian asking for Joy, Gabe stood. "Let's make Brian happy. He'll be good for all of us."

Martha and Hap were making sandwiches. Joy walked into her mother's arms. "Don't cry, sweetie, you'll upset Brian, okay?" Joy sniffed and nodded.

"I'm helping Mom set the table, Joy."

"Good job. We might have to move outside though; we have so many people."

"I set up a card table outside. We'll serve in here and find our own places out there."

Martha had a plan, and Joy numbly agreed. She held her stomach. "I don't think I can eat."

"Does your tummy hurt? Maybe you're nervous. I get nervous sometimes. Why are you nervous, Joy?" Brian was full of questions.

"Brides get nervous, buddy."

"Okay. Are you nervous, Gabe?"

"A little." Gabe patted a chair. "C'mere. I've hardly seen you today."

Hap led the prayer, and folks split up—some to the deck and others staying in the kitchen.

"Gretchen is sending my pink dress overnight. I wore it to the charity ball. Dad says it looks nice. I'm glad yours came in last week."

"Thanks, Mom. You're a sport."

Brian crawled onto Gabe's lap. Maybe he was getting too big for this, but Gabe figured they had other things to worry about. He rubbed the boy's back, realizing tension was leaving his body. Brian had picked up on something. Gabe dropped a kiss on the little fellow's raven hair.

"I'm surprised he hasn't gotten a military cut. He tries to do everything you do. He even shrugs like you do." Joy looked at the boy fondly.

"We're pretty tight, aren't we, kiddo?" Gabe agreed. Joy put her finger to her lips to hush him. Martha took Hap's hand and looked over at Gabe, where Brian had fallen asleep on his lap.

"He's not used to so many people," Gabe continued, softer. "He's worn out. Me, too. I was up all night organizing and getting the guys out. We have thirty men patrolling the perimeter of the farm. Nothing like the military to protect and defend. Someone said they were going to call in some motorcycle guys, too."

"I'm relying on God. But He's the One sending those people, isn't He?" Joy reached out to take Gabe's other hand—the one that was not on Brian's back. "Do you want to lay him down?"

"Not in your room, and he's too heavy to lug to the cottage. I'll carry him to the chaise on the deck. Let me fill out these papers, Pastor. We don't want to keep you all day. Thanks for what you've done." Pastor Davis handed Joy her papers and helped Gabe with his, shoving them over for him to sign. Then Gabe carried Brian to the deck and lay down with him on the chaise. Within minutes, he was asleep, too.

William looked over at Joy. "Now that he's part of the band, we can't work without him. But we could go over your vocals."

"Why don't we declare this a rest day? It's so crazy over here. I'll walk to the cottage and lie down."

"I'll come with you." William stood, and together they walked to Gabe and Brian's place. William scrolled on his phone while Joy went inside. Within an hour, her shrill cries split the air. William jumped up and rushed to the bedroom. Joy was hysterical, and Gabe appeared within minutes. She pointed to a pile of clothes beside the bed.

"What is this?" Gabe demanded.

"He was here. He was . . ." She made a motion with her hand.

"He was jacking off?" William asked. She nodded, sobbing. Gabe swore, and he took her into his arms. William laughed. "He took off naked as a jaybird then! Won't he have fun running through the woods with no clothes on?"

Gabe glared at him. "This isn't funny!" He thumbed his phone, calling the guardhouse to give them an alert. "We need to find out how this guy got in," he said into the phone. "He must have been watching and saw her come to my place." He walked over to the window. "No, it isn't locked. She must have opened it when she came in." Joy clung to him, saying she had opened it to get a breeze. Hap found them in the bedroom, and William filled him in while Gabe tried to quiet her.

Gabe hung up the phone. "We've got everyone looking for the breach, baby. I'm not letting you out of my sight, period."

"But the wedding isn't until Friday, Gabe."

"I don't care."

"I'll get Martha to come over and change the sheets," Hap suggested.

William caught sight of Brian and squatted down beside him. "Joy's okay, my man. She just had a nightmare."

"But it's daytime."

"It's what we call a bad dream. She had a bad dream."

"Okay. Joy?"

Joy sat down on the bed and opened her arms but quickly jumped up, remembering. "Can we get out of here?"

"We'll change the sheets, honey."

"Don't wash them, Hap," Gabe advised. "We don't want to destroy evidence." Joy trembled again, and Gabe led her to the living room.

Brian trailed after them, singing, "God has not given us a spirit of fear," repeating it twice and asking Gabe how the rest of it went.

"But of power, love, and a sound mind. Thanks, Bri. I'm glad

I learned that at Bible school with you last month. It's a perfect song right now."

"Miss Darlene said to sing it whenever we are afraid. Don't be afraid, Joy. We'll take care of you."

She opened her arms. "And God never fails us, does He? When all this is over, we should make a children's album—songs to make children brave and strong."

"And happy, because the joy of the Lord . . ." He looked at Gabe.

"Is our strength," Gabe finished.

"All what is over, Joy?" the boy asked.

"The nightmare," she replied.

"Read her the Shepherd's Psalm, Gabe. And the other one, about the secret place." Sitting beside Joy on the couch with one arm around her, Gabe pulled Brian to him with his other arm and recited Psalm 23 and Psalm 91.

Hap watched the three of them and then declared he was going to get Martha to change the sheets. "William, why don't you lock the windows, and we'll give this family some privacy?"

"Right on it, sir."

Gabe's phone rang. He untangled himself from Joy. "He's gone? Leave the tire tracks undisturbed. Save them for evidence." Gabe looked at his brother. "Would you please get Joy something to drink, buddy?"

Brian ran to the kitchen, giving Gabe enough time to explain they had found a breach in the fence where the property line turned the corner nearest the house but that the intruder had already gotten away. His phone rang again. It was the front gate reporting someone had tried to deliver flowers for the wedding and that a check-in with the house indicated no one there had ordered flowers. "I thought it was suspicious, some dude trying to deliver flowers in a minivan, but we didn't get a license plate," the front gate further detailed.

"Check the camera to see if you got a shot of it," Gabe suggested. They did have a photo of the minivan but nothing on the plate. "I need to call Pastor Davis. Can you hang on to him a while, Joy?"

"I'll go over to the house with him."

"Wait a sec, and I'll be right with you." Gabe went back to his room. He put some shells in his pocket and carried his rifle. "We saw more paw prints, buddy, so I figure the daddy bear came around looking for his mate."

"But you'll shoot him, too, won't ya, Gabe?"

"Maybe the wildlife guys can relocate him, Bri."

"Okay."

Martha and Hap came over to change the bedding. Hap said they would be careful to preserve evidence. Gabe, Brian, and Joy returned to the main house. Gabe, keeping a watchful eye on Joy, walked to a corner of the deck and leaned his rifle there. He called the pastor and filled him in while Joy cuddled with Brian, reading Peter Cottontail.

Gabe was firm—he would in no way let Joy out of his sight until this was over. He asked the pastor to call Dr. Wells to see if he could make a house call. Meanwhile, Dave and Stan challenged Brian to a game of fish and dealt the game around the kitchen table. "Nice guys in your band, Joy," Gabe observed. "I can't believe Brian is doing so well with them. But he didn't take to your sisters. I'm sorry about that. He's had too many new people. But he likes your mom, because she looks like you."

"He did okay with Daddy last night, too. He called him Pop."

"How are you doing?" Gabe asked. Joy held out her hands, which were shaking like leaves in an autumn wind. "I can't believe this happened. I'm so sorry."

"It's not your fault, Gabe. God is giving me lessons about mean people. I'll never be naïve again."

"Come here." Gabe held out his hand and led her to the chaise where he had been snoozing so peacefully less than an hour ago, unaware of the lurking danger. Pulling her down beside him, he asked if he could kiss her.

"Please." She clung to him. He gathered her still-trembling hands in his and kissed them tenderly. Hearing the ongoing game of fish, the couple walked into the kitchen to watch.

"Brian is ruthless about more than honesty, Gabe—look at all those tricks. He remembers who has the card he wants."

"And you don't give him a clue, right?" Gabe winked. Hearing the gate chime, Gabe learned Pastor Davis was there with Dr. Wells. "Dr. Wells is coming to see you, Bri."

"Why? He's never been here before."

"I invited him. Is that okay?"

"No."

"He likes Joy. He met her a couple of weeks ago, remember?"

"Oh, yeah. Why can't we go to his office?"

"Maybe next week."

"He's nice, Joy. You could tell him about your daymare."

Gabe greeted the two arriving men, and Dave scooped up the cards, saying maybe they could play later. Dr. Wells wanted to find a place where Brian would be most comfortable, and Gabe, holding firmly to Joy's hand, led him downstairs, where they found William playing drums. William took off the headphones, and Gabe made introductions. Dr. Wells noted he had heard all about the drummer with the "dreadful" locks.

William rubbed his short hair. "Things are a little crazy around here. We could use a shrink and a pastor. I'll turn the drums over to my man so you can watch him play. See ya later, my man."

"Gabe and Joy need to talk about getting married, Brian. Are you ready to share Gabe with Joy?"

"Joy loves me, Dr. Wells."

"How does that feel?"

"Good. Two people love me, like Mama and Dad did. And she doesn't care that I'm difficult."

"So, we can let them figure out getting married, and you can show me the drums?" Brian put the headphones on the patient doctor and played—not too bad—while the pastor and the couple went upstairs.

They sat in the living room with Joy's parents. Martha said she wanted the wedding to happen that day so Gabe could always keep an eye on Joy, reminding the pastor he was a sniper. Gabe was relieved when Pastor Davis said he could sign the marriage papers on Friday. "Let's move the couch against the back wall and set up some chairs. I brought some from the church."

They counted out members of the family and of the band, setting up the necessary number of chairs. Joy went to put on her dress, and Hap ran to the cottage to get Gabe's suit, knowing Gabe would not leave her long enough to do that himself. Leaning his rifle in a corner of the kitchen, Gabe texted the guys to get ready for a wedding, and he stepped into the half bath to put his suit on before sending Hap to get Brian.

Dr. Wells sat beside Brian, and Gabe stood in front of the pastor. The guys and Martha and Hap sat in the front rows. Dave started some music, and Joy's sisters came down the aisle, one by one. Brian told Dr. Wells he did not like them because they thought they owned Joy. "It's hard to share, isn't it, Brian?"

When all was quiet, Dave started the music again, and Joy walked down the aisle. She was calm and purposeful, keeping her eyes fixed on Gabe. He took her hand, whispering, "You're so beautiful you make my heart break." Hap stood when Pastor Davis asked who giveth this woman. He answered that he and her mother did.

"Dearly beloved . . ." The ceremony began. Although the pastor did not rush, and he even gave a little homily, it was over quickly, and Gabe took Joy in his arms and kissed her. He put his forehead on hers.

"I'm sorry about all this, Joy."

"I'm not sorry. I'm married. To you."

Gabe gazed into her cornflower blue eyes and took her hands, which were no longer trembling. "I love you, Joy."

"And I love you."

Pastor Davis announced that he and Dr. Wells brought cake from Bonnie Bell. He said if the bride and groom would come cut it, everyone could enjoy it, which they did. Dr. Wells then pulled Gabe aside and told him Brian had indeed picked up on the anxiety and was worried about Joy, insisting something was wrong. "I called a psychiatrist and discussed it with him. Hopefully, this will be a short-term thing and this stalker will be brought to justice. But we are giving you five mild children's sedatives to get Brian through this. Use at your discretion."

"Brian and I couldn't have made it without you, Dr. Wells. Thanks for coming by the house."

"Joy is doing you both as much good as I did." Dr. Wells

clapped him on the back and left with Pastor Davis.

"Now I need to do two more things. First, we need to brush hog behind my cottage. Any of you musicians good for stuff like that?" Stan volunteered, saying his dad had a farm. Gabe directed him to the barn to get equipment. Meanwhile, Martha and Hap had brought their suitcases with them, and they were setting themselves up in Joy's bedroom.

"Where are you going to sleep, Joy?" Brian wondered aloud. She blushed.

"Joy and I got married, buddy. She's going to sleep at our place."

"Oh, like Mama and Dad. In your bed, right?"

"Yep."

"Okay. That's good."

"Hopefully, he'll get a chance to destroy one of the stalker's crazy fantasies," Dave muttered under his breath.

Much as I like that idea, Gabe thought, *it won't be possible tonight after her trauma today. I've never wanted to take out a bad guy as much as I want to take out this one!*

"Joy, you married my brother. Does that make you my sister?"

One of Joy's sisters, Megan, told Brian it did and that it made him brother to all the Thomas sisters. "Now we are one family, right Mom?"

Brian studied her. "Okay. That's good."

"Can I have a hug then?"

"Maybe later." Brian shrugged, and everybody laughed.

"He looks just like Gabe when he does that." Joy looked at Gabe, who shrugged, causing everyone to laugh again. "What's the second thing you need to do, Gabe?"

"Get out of this suit." Hap was now gathering up plates and

cups, stuffing them into plastic bags. He caught Gabe's eye and nodded toward the rifle, suggesting he reclaim it. "Good, Hap. Thanks." Gabe grabbed it, and he was in and out of the little bathroom in less than five minutes, tucking his shirt in. "Where's Joy?"

"Mom and Grace are helping her change. She looked pretty, didn't she?" Megan asked.

"Took my breath away." When Joy came out of the bedroom, Gabe said he wanted to see how Stan was coming along with the mowing behind the cottage. She reached out her hand to him. Gripping the rifle, he went onto the deck, checking out the perimeter before leading her down the stairs.

Wordlessly, they walked over to the cottage, but Gabe did not go inside yet. Instead, he veered around back, noting Stan had cleared about ten feet and was continuing. Gabe waved encouragement and swept his eyes around the perimeter again. Fiddling with his belt, he pulled out a walkie-talkie and asked the guys at the front gate if everything was quiet. They gave him the all clear.

Dropping on the deck's couch, Gabe pulled Joy down beside him, thinking, *Is she really my wife now?* He heard the noise of the brush hog and of birds singing. *Good, if birds are singing, no one is creeping up on us.* Gabe could not turn off thinking like a sniper; he had been one for almost a decade while he was in Special Forces.

The sun was shining brightly—*Poor Stan, the heat must be brutal*—and he relaxed a bit, knowing how much the guys in the band loved Joy. He was not alone in this fight. He nudged her, pointing at a chipmunk running along the banister. She leaned against him, and he held her hands out. *No tremors. Brave girl.* She looked up at him with those cornflower blue eyes, and he kissed her.

Hearing someone clumsy running, Gabe looked up. Brian was making his way toward them. "Is Joy okay?" he wanted to know. Joy patted the seat beside her, and when he sat, she pulled him close. "Got your rifle, Gabe?" His brother pointed to it, not five feet away, leaning against the corner. "And your shells?" He patted his pocket. "You aren't worried about the daddy bear, are you? Someone wants to hurt Joy, but you won't let him. Why would anyone want to hurt Joy?"

Why did I think I could fool him? "She's a good person, buddy. And evil hates good." The boy's face pulled into a frown. "But we won't let him hurt her."

"Okay."

"I've got an idea, buddy. We can make ice cream."

The trio made their way back to the house. Gabe found the electric churn in the pantry, Martha made the fixings with all the extra cream they had bought for the cubs, and they set up on the deck. Gabe went out first, listening to the birds. *How could evil stalk beauty? This is My Father's world.* He did not realize he had begun singing out loud until Joy's voice joined him—"I rest me in the thought. All nature sings and 'round me rings, the music of the spheres."

Martha joined them on the deck. "Your voices sound lovely together."

"God brought you together," Hap added. He rested his hand on Brian's hair.

"Do you think I'm difficult, Pop? Dad thought I was difficult."

"Difficult? No, I haven't seen it."

"You've grown up a lot since Mom and Dad died, buddy."

"I don't want to be difficult."

"Help me pour the salt in this ice." Gabe heard the silence and reached for his rifle, but it was just Stan coming.

"How far back should I go? I cleared fifteen feet or so."

"That should do it. Take a load off. We're making ice cream."

"Gabe won't let anyone hurt Joy, Stan," Brian said, filling him in.

"The kid's too smart for his own good," Stan observed, and Gabe agreed with a nod. "I'll catch a shower and join the guys."

"I'll come watch."

When Stan stared at Brian, Joy informed him, "That's a high compliment. He watches Gabe shower."

"But people like their privacy, Bri."

"Okay. I won't."

"Besides, I need your help, Brian. We need to find the bowls," Martha explained, reaching out her hand. "Come show me where they are."

"We need enough for the sisters. Where are the sisters, Mom?" Brian went cheerfully after her.

"Where are they?" Gabe looked around.

"Watching TV, Gabe. Safe in the living room." Hap pointed.

"Good."

Joy went into the kitchen to help her mother gather bowls and spoons, and then she called her sisters to join everyone on the deck. Gabe heard her and automatically scanned the perimeter again. Hap watched him. "Old habits die hard, don't they? How long were you a sniper?"

"Almost a decade."

"Mostly in Iraq?"

"And Afghanistan. I had a few leaves, hanging around here

to see Brian and the folks." Gabe shook his head. "I know this property, Hap. I was stupid to build on the edge of the woods." Hap snorted. "No one would ever have thought of this scenario, Gabe. No one. This is bizarre." Then, changing the subject, he noted, "That churn is slowing down—maybe it's ready." They lifted the lid, and the sisters returned with the bowls.

Brian carried chocolate sauce, with a triumphant grin. He held it high over his bowl, but Gabe lifted the bowl to catch it, warning him not to spill. "Was that difficult, Gabe?"

"Not really, Bri. Just a little inappropriate."

"Okay."

The girls exclaimed over how delicious the ice cream was, and Brian offered them chocolate sauce to make it even better. "That was appropriate, Gabe. I shared."

"And I'm really proud of you, buddy."

When Brian grinned his lopsided grin, chocolate escaped his mouth. Seeing the boy's chocolate face, Martha brought Gabe a washcloth and watched him wipe the boy's mouth and cheeks, pronouncing him, "All clean."

"It's getting dark," Gabe realized. "We should all get inside. Hap, will you check the windows and doors? Are my people ready to go?"

"Joy is going to sleep in Gabe's bed. They got married," Brian remembered.

Gabe chuckled when Joy put her hands on her blushing face. "You give new meaning to the phrase 'blushing bride,' Joy." He took her hand, and they stood and watched Hap as he locked the door and waved goodnight.

When they got to the caretaker's cottage in the gathering dusk, Gabe unlocked the front door and asked Brian to hold it open. He swept his bride up in his arms, and he carried her across the threshold. When Brian asked why, he told him that is what grooms do.

"I'm going to check the place," Gabe decided. And he did—every door and window was locked. Brian looked in the closets and under the bed, but Gabe suddenly halted him when he noticed their Mom and Dad's spread on his bed. He had asked Martha and Hap to keep his usual spread unwashed to preserve evidence of the intruder, and they must have found this one in a closet at the house. They had even hung the matching curtains.

Gabe swung around to catch his brother, but Brian said, "That's appropriate, Gabe. Mama and Dad's stuff in your married room, because you married Joy."

Tears stung Gabe's eyes, and he drew the boy into a hug. "Are you sharing again, Bri?"

"No, you are. But Mama and Dad are happy you married Joy. Do we need to shower?"

"Not tonight, buddy. We can say the Blesseds. How about that?"

"And the Secret Place."

"And the Shepherd's Psalm, too." Joy patted Brian's bed, signaling him over.

Gabe spoke them all from memory. "Are you too big to rock?"

"Not too big tonight. Maybe next night." So big brother carried him out to the rocker in the living room, moving him back and forth until he dozed off. He then tucked the boy into bed, dropping a kiss on his brow. Brian never stirred.

Joy waited in the living room, and Gabe dropped beside her on the couch. "I know this has been a traumatic day for you, and I want you to know I don't expect anything. We'll let you heal from this morning's ordeal."

"Can *I* watch you shower?"

"I'd rather shower *with* you." He was concerned, however, because the rush of the ceremony had not allowed him time to buy protection. "But I don't have . . . protection, Joy."

"That's all right. I want to make a baby with you."

"You do?"

"Mm-hmm."

He did not know if they made a baby, but he gave it his best effort. It was not that he was eager to destroy the stalker's fantasies—he was simply eager.

CHAPTER 12

The Day after the Wedding

JOY WAS SINGING, and it woke Gabe. "Hi, sleepyhead. Did I wake you?"

The sun was bright, and Brian was moving around. "What time is it?" Gabe leaned up to check the clock. "Good grief. Fine protector I am."

"I already answered the guardhouse twice. No sign of him. The guards have been around the perimeter once every half an hour, night and day. I'd say you're keeping us safe, soldier."

"Where'd you get clothes?"

"Daddy brought my suitcase to me." She blushed. "He asked what I wore last night, and I told him your T-shirt worked fine."

Gabe grinned. "But it was better when I got it off." She blushed again, and he chuckled. "My blushing bride. What's Brian up to?"

"He's got a foam bullet gun, and he's shooting targets. He was fine as soon as he saw you, but he asked if you were naked. I told him you have your bottoms on."

In a chorus, they both answered, "And he said, 'okay.'"

They laughed at this, and Joy added, "I love that little scamp." She handed Gabe his jeans, and he got dressed. As he pulled a

103

T-shirt over his head, he found Brian in the kitchen, who had set out eggs and bacon.

"Waiting for me, buddy?"

"You cook breakfast good."

Gabe rang the guardhouse. No sign of the stalker, so he set about making eggs and bacon. Joy came in, looking beautiful and relaxed. He drew her into his arms and kissed her. She pulled back. "Don't burn the bacon."

"Okay," he said, sounding like Brian. They laughed again. After they ate, he asked Joy if her dad could shoot. She said he was no sniper but that he managed to get at least one deer every season and had asked about coming to the farm for hunting season. "We've got a lot of deer on the farm. But, more importantly, I should have given him a rifle last night. I'll get one out of the gun cabinet today. I bet Stan shoots, too, if his dad owns a farm in Tennessee."

"Dad said he saw an eight-point on the way over."

"I hate that everybody is stuck inside. It's so beautiful here."

Brian wanted to go to the big house, because the guys said they would play fish with him. Gabe stepped out of the cottage first and listened, sweeping the perimeter with his eyes before opening the door and waving them out. He carried his rifle like he always did, pointing down, while his eyes constantly checked out both sides as they walked.

As soon as they got to the house, Gabe gathered all the men together, asking them about their shooting abilities. As he figured, Hap and Stan were hunters, Rocky and Dave not so much, and William had an aversion to guns. He waved them to the hallway closet and gave them their choice of weapons. Hap chose Gabe's father's rifle, saying he hunted with one like it, and Stan chose

Gabe's old hunting rifle.

Reaching up to the shelf, Gabe pulled down materials for cleaning. He told Stan his rifle tended to pull left and that he could show him how to overcome it. He set up a target off the back deck, called the gate to tell them they would be doing some target practice, and then let the guys have at it. Hap was a good shooter, no surprise there. But Gabe gave him a few pointers to improve his ability. Stan watched and learned, too, and Gabe took his old gun and adjusted the scope while coaching him as well.

Seeing sun reflecting off glass across the road, Gabe sensed trouble, and he moved everyone inside. Once there, he went for his father's binoculars.

"What is it, Gabe?"

Standing in the doorway, he told Hap and Stan someone was watching them from across the road. He called the guardhouse and urged the guards to be cautious in checking it out. "I don't want him to know I spotted him." Tom, at the guardhouse, had been an Army Ranger. He contacted the local sheriff, and the two of them examined some tire tracks on the property. The sheriff took the soiled bedspread with him as evidence when he left, finding nothing else out of place at the time.

"This must be the most exciting thing to happen in Lost Creek in years, Gabe," Hap commented.

"A guy murdered an old lady for drug money last year."

"Why is it called Lost Creek? How can you lose a creek?" Stan wanted to know.

Gabe chuckled. "When they tried to find its source, it ran into a mountain—a hill really. But it never came out the other side. Probably an underground aquifer."

"I lived here a long time, so I know that's a true story," Hap affirmed.

Gabe's walkie-talkie went off, and one of the guards told him the mail had arrived and that one letter, in particular, might prove interesting. Gabe did not want to leave Joy, so Stan volunteered to walk down and get it. Joy started onto the porch, but Gabe grabbed her. "Someone's watching again." But when he took a second look, he saw no reflection anymore. *Where was he?*

Tom called, saying he believed he had not been discovered and that the guy had left. "He's a greenhorn, though. Left a trail plain as day. Me and Avery are going after him."

God, please let them get him. Let this be over.

Stan handed Gabe an envelope. "This was in the mailbox. It was stuck in there with no stamp."

Gabe went into the house and came back with a cloth napkin. "Probably ten hands have handled this already, but . . ." He opened the envelope, scanned the note inside quickly, and handed it to Hap, who then read it himself.

So, you beat me. Was it good for you? But I see two other little morsels over there. Joy comes from pretty stock, but I'm not through with her yet.

Hap swore. "We'll get him, Hap. The guys are tracking him now—said he's a greenhorn and left a trail plain as day," Gabe assured him. But soon, the report came back. The stalker had indeed driven away. The nightmare continued.

Rocky poked his head out the door. "Have we entirely given up work? Can we get anything done?"

Stan allowed as how he needed at least a gallon of water first but, after that, would be game. Hearing Dave already practicing with his flute, Gabe locked the door, set the deadbolt, and led the way downstairs. "You're their mascot, Bri, and they'll let you listen."

"We're mainly practicing," Rocky said. "Do the girls want to come?" They were with Joy, and she ushered them downstairs. Gabe and Hap arranged chairs, and they, Martha, and the girls enjoyed the practice. It was interrupted by a perimeter check, but all was clear. The guards could tell the stalker had driven off toward town.

Martha suggested a lunch break, but Gabe went upstairs first and stepped out onto the deck to listen and sweep his eyes across the property. Hap came out. "All quiet?"

"Yes, sir."

"Martha told me last night she is proud of you. We all feel safe."

"I didn't keep Joy safe yesterday. I screwed up badly on that, and I'm so sorry."

"Didn't take you long to build a fortress."

"But he breached it, Hap, and I missed it."

"Don't beat yourself up. She looks pretty happy now."

Gabe averted his eyes. "I did tell her I'd give her time to heal from the ordeal, but . . ."

Hap chuckled. "Yep, she looks pretty healed now."

"Did you know that you and Martha put Mom and Dad's spread on the bed?"

"I never thought. Did Brian see?"

"Yeah, and he said it was 'appropriate' to have their married things in there because we are married."

"He's not difficult—he's a treasure."

"Dr. Wells has done a lot with him. And Joy has, too."

"And you, Gabe." Gabe shrugged. "When this is over, we'll send you two on a nice honeymoon."

"Will have to be a honeymoon for three—I doubt Joy would leave Brian any more than I would. I think they're ready. Are you hungry?"

Martha and Hap were interested in the band's music. After all, she sang in the church choir, and Hap directed it. So they sat around discussing each band member's history with his instruments, and they wanted to know how Gabe had learned the guitar. Rocky told them how they discovered Gabe's talents and about Gabe saying he merely "fooled around" with it.

Gabe shrugged. "I'm no performer. I'm waiting for the bloom to fall off the roses. Joy still needs a professional."

Joy put her hands on her hips. "I've found my professional." Gabe shook his head.

"Professional at what?" Dave asked with a wink.

"Professional guitarist, singer, and songwriter." Joy still had her hands on her hips.

"How about lover?" Stan suggested. She blushed.

"How about sniper?" from Hap.

"He makes a good breakfast," Brian put in his favorite.

"Let's get back to work." Checking the lock on the door after doing his perimeter sweep, Gabe went downstairs, and the others followed.

CHAPTER 13

All Is Quiet

THE SHERIFF'S DEPARTMENT called Gabe the next day to report it had located the minivan at a hotel nearby. The vehicle had a Tennessee license plate, which gave them the name of the driver. But he checked out of the hotel after the sheriff questioned him. Gabe thanked the sheriff and assured him he would not give up taking care of Joy.

"The sheriff thinks he found the car," Gabe reported. "But the guy checked out of the hotel after they questioned him. He's our man, but he's at large." Nevertheless, they neither saw nor heard any indication of him the entire day, and some of the guys on patrol began to ease up. A few of them even abandoned their perimeter search, figuring the guy had left town.

Gabe maintained his vigilance. The remaining guards at the front gate maintained their vigilance, too. The day crawled by, and everyone was a bit on edge, but Gabe could not ask the volunteers to walk the perimeter night and day. Joy said they should have paid them more, though it was too late now. She insisted on paying those who remained, however.

On Friday, they got back in stride and worked hard. Rocky felt some of the new songs were ready to produce. Pastor Davis popped in with the marriage papers, having Joy, Gabe, and witnesses sign them. He took them down to the courthouse and said he hoped they never heard from the stalker again. Gabe remained skeptical about that prospect.

"I'm not ready to leave you until we have some sort of resolution," Hap confessed. He continued to take time off from work. And on Saturday, he and Martha ran out to the store to resupply the house.

Although they did not try to go to church—settling instead for gathering for devotions—by afternoon, Gabe figured they could venture out for a walk. He hated that Joy's family had not seen the entire beautiful farm yet. Brian checked to make sure his brother had his rifle and held tightly to Joy's hand as they began their walk.

Gabe stopped, and he held his hand up to caution everyone. "Someone is following us," he whispered, looking around for a place to hide.

"Go to the bear cave," Joy suggested.

Urging quiet, Gabe herded them beyond the stream and into the cave, which went farther back than he thought. Even the usually-chattering girls were now silent as they smashed back as far as they could. Gabe stayed near the front, listening. He moved back as someone approached. Gabe whispered that when whoever it was following them stopped to look inside, he would make a noise like a bear. He then went ahead and made the noise, sounding so much like a bear that the girls grabbed hold of each other.

The person outside the cave stopped and backed up a bit. Gabe growled again, deep in his throat, and he was surprised to hear an answering growl! *Was it a bear following them?* Then they heard a scream, and he realized that, no—whoever had been following them was jumped by a bear! The screams continued, and Gabe advanced to see a pudgy man lying on the ground on his back with a bear on top biting and clawing him.

"Roll over, mister! Cover your head!" The bear spun around and stared at Gabe but then returned to his victim, who had not moved. "I can't get a shot off," Gabe said. So he shot in the air instead, and the bear ran off. "Whoever he is, he's no threat anymore," Gabe informed the others. "I'm going to run to the house and call an ambulance. Hap, you and Stan move everyone out of here and don't look. It's not a pretty sight. Hang on to your rifle, Hap. That bear is out there somewhere. Bri, take care of Joy."

He took off, and he was out of sight by the time everyone else exited the cave. Dave and Stan put the bleeding man on an improvised stretcher while Rocky tried to stem the bleeding. William went over to some nearby bushes and vomited. Brian clung to Joy, but Hap told him not to move far because the bear was still out there and had tasted blood. Dave and Stan hoisted the stretcher, and Rocky walked beside them, still doing his best to lessen the bleeding.

Gabe ran back to them. "The ambulance is on its way." He checked for the man's pulse, and he shook his head, indicating he could find none. "I doubt he'll make it." Before the EMTs arrived, men showed up from the guardhouse to report they had found the minivan during a perimeter sweep. "Be careful guys. A bear got him, and it's still out there." Every man drew his weapon, but the bear was already long gone.

Gabe was proud of the Thomas women. Martha had moved up to hold Hap's hand once the reinforcements arrived, and Joy was calm. "Nice Sunday stroll, right?" The sisters giggled at Gabe, albeit with an edge of hysteria.

Someone had called the sheriff, and he met them at the house. He identified the injured man as the stalker, and when the EMTs arrived, they pronounced the man dead. Gabe said they needed to get the Department of Natural Resources to track the bear because it needed to be put down. The sheriff said he would get right on it, and then he shook his head toward Gabe. "Can't put down that sniper rifle yet, Mr. Winslow."

They would have spent another housebound day, but a couple of band members wanted to take the girls out to a movie and dinner. Gabe thought maybe they had designs on the sisters. But he knew they just needed a little fun either way.

"I hope they see a good romantic comedy and get their minds off this disastrous day," Joy mentioned.

"At least it's all over, baby. And, by the way, I think Rocky likes Grace."

"And Dave is interested in Megan."

"You think so? What do your folks think about the guys in your band having 'the hots' for your sisters?"

"They like all the guys in my band, but Dad has most in common with Stan. Why don't we take Stan, William, and Dave to Minards for dinner?"

Gabe, Joy, and Brian took everyone to the Italian restaurant for dinner. All the talk was about the ordeal they had survived. And Brian wanted to know why the wildlife guys could not just take the daddy bear somewhere else, as Gabe had suggested. Gabe explained that once a bear had tasted a human, it was not safe around people anymore.

"Two dumb men caused the destruction of two beautiful wild animals. I hate that," Gabe said, with disappointment. "But we saved the babies, and they'll be returned to the wild. They took them to a guy who has a refuge in the southern part of the state. He has all kinds of animals—baby bears, birds, injured animals. He rehabilitates them and then turns them loose. I'll show you on the computer when we get home." Brian had more spaghetti on him than in him, and Gabe wiped his face with a napkin. "Did you like that, buddy?"

"It's better than you make."

"It doesn't come out of a can, Bri."

"How do they make it?"

Joy laughed. "I'll show you next week. We'll make some. I never cook spaghetti from a can. Ugh!"

"But I make good breakfast," Gabe teased.

"Gabe makes good breakfast," Brian confirmed.

Everyone laughed and then stood to leave. Martha looped her arm in Gabe's. "I don't know how to thank you for keeping my baby safe—for keeping all of us safe."

"I don't know how I fell in love with her so quickly, but one day she came down my driveway with a song on her lips and walked straight into my heart. I'm so sorry I let that pervert get into my place. Father, forgive me, but I'm glad he's dead."

Hap and Gabe argued over the bill, but William settled it, surprising them with the news that "Winslow Farm" was now ranked best-selling single. Joy put the meal on *her* card.

Back at the farm, the group split up at the main house, and Gabe pulled the truck down to the cottage. Brian was already asleep, and Joy unlocked the cottage door so Gabe could carry him inside. He tucked Brian in, dropping a kiss on his unresponsive brow.

"Want to take a shower?" Joy suggested with a kiss. "You know I have 'the hots' for you, baby."

Gabe reached for Joy. She turned in his arms, and she drew him down for a long, lingering kiss, to which he responded enthusiastically. She ran her hands down his body, to which his body responded enthusiastically. *Married life is a good thing!* "I love you, baby. And I'm going to show you how much."

Hearing a light tapping on the door, Gabe raised his head. Struggling into his shorts, he threw Joy his T-shirt and cracked the door. "Not appropriate, buddy, to knock on married people's door."

"Can I sleep with you? Mama let me sleep with her."

"No wonder Dad called you difficult," he muttered.

"But I'm scared, Gabe."

Joy raised her head. "Why are you scared, Brian?"

"B . . . be . . . bec . . . because it was so much blood. When the mean man who hurt you . . . Did he die?"

Joy held out her arms, and Brian flung himself at her. She held him close and rubbed his back. "He did. He'll never hurt us again."

"But he didn't go to be with Mama and Dad because Jesus didn't live in his heart."

Gabe sat on the edge of the bed and dropped his head. He put his hand on Brian's shoulder. "I'm sorry, buddy. I'm sorry you saw that. Come here." He patted the bed between them, and Brian scooted closer. Brian abandoned Joy's arms and tucked himself into his brother's safe embrace, and he cried heartbroken sobs until he fell asleep.

* * *

In the morning, Gabe washed the dried tears from Brian's face and invited him to help cook breakfast. When Brian was getting more eggs out of the bowl than in it, Gabe grabbed some bread and suggested he make toast. They worked side by side.

"I'm sorry I was difficult last night."

"You weren't difficult, Bri. Just a little inappropriate."

"But you said I was difficult."

"I was cross and tired, buddy, and I'm sorry for that. Forgive me?"

Intently buttering the toast, crumbling it when the hard butter would not spread, Brian shrugged. "Okay."

"Thanks. I love you, Bri."

The toast in the boy's mouth spewed when he replied, "I love you, too, Gabe." Gabe put a napkin under a stream of warm water, wiped Brian's face, and drew him into his arms. "But why was I not appropriate last night?"

"Married people need privacy, Bri."

"Okay." After a pause, he added, "Why?"

Placing a plate on the table, Gabe pointed. "Eat." He sat beside him, digging into his own eggs.

"Why?"

Gabe placed his hands over his face and took a deep breath. "They just do, that's all." Brian looked at him with confusion on his face. "Look, didn't you tell William you want a baby?"

"Yep. Because you got married."

"Married people need privacy to make a baby."

"Oh. How do you do that?"

Gabe rubbed his hands over his face. "I have to plant a seed."

"Be sure to put your jacket on."

"Put my jacket on?"

"Yeah. It's cold in the garden at night."

Gabe caught sight of Joy putting her hand over her mouth and fleeing back to the bedroom. *Coward*, he thought. "Uh, today is Tuesday. So why don't we talk to Dr. Wells about this?"

"You don't know where to plant the seed?"

"I've got a pretty good idea. But it requires privacy, Bri. If you want a baby, you have to give us privacy."

"I can't watch?"

"Nope." Seeing Joy giggling again, Gabe waved her in. "Come on. Do you want some eggs?" When she nodded, he added, "If you can contain your mirth, have a seat."

"May I please have some bacon?"

"Bacon, Gabe. You forgot the bacon," Brian exclaimed in shock.

"I guess his mind was on other things, Brian. But he didn't forget the toast. You have lots of toast."

"*I* made it."

"Scrambled or fried, Joy?" Gabe offered to cook the eggs for her.

"With all this toast, I'll have one over hard, and I'll make a sandwich—if you know where to put it that is," Joy teased.

Gabe leaned down, gave her a kiss, and whispered, "If you keep him out of our bed, I'll show you exactly where to put it." She blushed.

"Gabe?"

Gabe took the plate Brian had rinsed and put it in the dishwasher. "What, buddy?"

"If you have a pretty good idea, what is it?"

Dear God, I'm not ready for this! "I need to put the seed inside of Joy, because a baby needs nine months to grow in her tummy."

"Oh. How do you do that?"

Joy got up and turned the bacon. "Brian, we need to focus. I don't want burned bacon."

"Oh. Yeah."

"After we eat our bacon, we need to go work with the band, okay?" After slicing some tomato for Joy's sandwich, Gabe made himself a bacon, egg, and tomato sandwich as well. The conversation had worked up his appetite.

They filled the dishwasher and headed over to the main house. After hugs and kisses, Joy's family pulled off, headed for Nashville. Hap shook hands with Gabe, thanking him again for taking care of his girl.

Joy played some of the band's videos for Brian, and the band worked until lunchtime. Word about the stalker's demise had gotten back to the office in Nashville, and the band's publicist, Monte, called to inform everyone the stalker was a well-known producer who had been accused of sexual advances on numerous young women trying to break into the industry. Stories about it were popping up everywhere, and Joy considered herself very fortunate.

After lunch, Gabe took Brian to Dr. Wells so they could further discuss the "seed" issue. The psychologist said Gabe had done a good job with him about it. Knowing the family was Christian, he gave some Christian books about it to Brian. He gave him second-grade reading level books, and he left a third-grade reading level book with Gabe for when more questions came up later. He reminded the boy they had talked about how hard it was to share Joy with Gabe, stressing the need for married folks to have privacy.

Gabe and Joy resolved to show Brian lots of love, and Gabe realized how blessed he was to have a wife who adored his little brother. Many evenings that summer, they sat on the deck and watched the stars come out, saying Psalm 91, the Shepherd's Psalm, and the Blesseds together as a family. Once Gabe carried Brian inside and kissed him goodnight, Brian usually stayed down for the night. Occasionally, when he did wake, Gabe took him to his and Joy's room.

They faced a big decision when the time for the Gospel Music Association Dove Awards drew near. "Winslow Farm" was nominated, but Gabe felt the occasion was too much for his brother, so he planned to stay home with him. But to Gabe's surprise, while the guys in the band were discussing it at lunch one day, Brian said he wanted to go. Even after they showed him some videos of past Dove Award events, he still wanted to go. Gabe warned him about the crowds, and he vowed to be appropriate. Gabe finally agreed, telling Joy he could take him back to the hotel if he could not handle it.

William, Rocky, and Dave set off in the van, with Stan following in his truck. Before William left, Brian hugged him, and the drummer promised they would see each other in Nashville.

CHAPTER 14

The Dove Awards

GABE AND JOY FLEW out of Pittsburg with Brian, headed for Nashville and the Dove Awards. Brian had never flown before, and he was fascinated, exclaiming how small the cars were while the plane ascended. Gabe put his finger to his lips, and the boy lowered his volume. Big brother explained the cars looked smaller because the plane was flying so high. Soon, the cars disappeared altogether as the plane entered the clouds.

When the stewardess offered them something to drink, Brian asked Gabe how much it cost, and Joy told him the price was included in the ticket. Gabe suggested a Coke, but Joy said to bring him a Shirley Temple. Brian was delighted with the fancy drink.

"He may not make it through the awards, but this experience is worth the price of admission." Gabe watched Brian, who had his eyes glued to the window, and he handed Brian's drink over to Joy to avoid the inevitable spill. Brian soon turned back, looking for his drink, and Gabe replaced it in front of him. When the boy pulled on his ears in discomfort, Joy suggested he swallow, and his eyes got large as his ears popped.

"Have you ever been on a plane, Gabe?" Brian wanted to know.

"Iraq and Afghanistan are across the ocean, Bri. I flew many times."

"Oh. Yeah. Dad showed me on the globe. How long did it take?"

"Too long. I couldn't wait to see you and the folks when flying home."

"Yeah. Once we drove up to meet you. You were surprised."

"I was."

"But you aren't going back ever again, are you? Because Mama and Dad aren't here."

"Nope. You're stuck with me, Bri."

"I'm glad."

Gabe put his arm around the boy, who would have climbed into his lap if he could; but the seatbelt sign was on. Glancing at Joy, he whispered, "He's getting too big for my lap, but I can't resist him."

She leaned her head against his shoulder, her golden locks spilling over it. "He needs your lap, Gabe."

Landing in Nashville was another adventure, and Brian plastered his face against the window. Gabe offered to wipe the window before they got off, but the stewardess assured him they would get it. Because of the boy's handicap, they were exited off the plane first.

Emerging from the security zone, they spotted Hap and Martha, and Brian ran to them. Hap grinned, and he asked Joy if she could top Brian's enthusiastic hugs. "I wouldn't even try. But I love you, Dad. Thanks for picking us up." Martha listened intently to Brian's rendition of their adventure on the plane.

With a wink, Hap shook Gabe's hand. "Good to see you, son."

They made the required bathroom stops—Brian explaining he wanted to be appropriate—and headed to collect their bags. The sisters would be waiting at the hotel, where Monte had arranged a dinner for everyone. Brian was disappointed because William was not at the airport. But he accepted Gabe's promise that William was in Nashville and they would see him soon.

After more hugs at the hotel, Gabe looked around at the beautiful suite reserved for them, noting the extra bedroom for Brian. He never traveled in such luxury as a soldier, but his wife was a rising star, nominated for a Dove Award. *How did this happen?*

Though glad to see Joy's parents, Brian would not let Martha help him change clothes, insisting on Gabe instead. So big brother did the honors and then sent him into the living room to wait. Joy stepped out of the bathroom in a blue dress her mother had purchased for her. Gabe's eyes widened with appreciation, and he tossed his suit on the bed to take her in his arms, murmuring how gorgeous she was. "I hope I don't have to use combat skills to keep the men away."

"You already did, remember?"

He shuddered. "Don't remind me," he said, and he kissed her. With a tap on the door, he disentangled himself from Joy, saying they would be there in a minute. He quickly got dressed. To his surprise, dinner was served in the suite. Monte greeted them there, thanking Gabe profusely for keeping Joy and the others safe and teasing him about his quick marriage. "When you save someone's life, you have to watch after her for the rest of her life. No choice," Gabe sighed.

Joy plunked her hands on her hips. "You wanted a choice, Gabe?"

"Nope."

"But you love her, Gabe."

"Yep, buddy." He winked. "Like I said, no choice. I have to stay married to her for the rest of our lives."

After Gabe dodged questions about the stalker throughout dinner, they learned plans for a rehearsal the next day. The band was scheduled to perform at the awards, and Brian was expected to be at the rehearsal. Once he learned William would be there, he was excited.

* * *

The next day, Brian dressed himself and pounded on Gabe and Joy's door at 6:00 a.m. Gabe informed him they did not need to be at rehearsal until nine o'clock but that they could get some breakfast for now. Joy told them to order room service.

They arrived at rehearsal fifteen minutes early. Brian could not wait to see William, who was there waiting for them, ready for the hug he fully expected and fully reciprocated. "How are you doing, my man? This is your instrument." He handed him a stick and a triangle.

"What do I do with it?"

William took the little stick and demonstrated. "Rocky will point to you at the appropriate time."

"I want to be appropriate."

"I know you do, my man."

"I don't want to mess up Joy's song."

"You won't. After Rocky points to you, he'll give you the signal to strike."

"Okay. I'll try."

"We'll practice."

So they did, and with only a few mistakes, Brian otherwise

played his part perfectly.

Gabe told Brian they would be out late that night, and he suggested a rest. They trooped up to their room, and Joy and Brian fell asleep. Gabe knew her early-stage pregnancy tired her, and he was surprised she had not announced it to one and all yet. He stretched out beside her, content with watching her sleep. But he had left the door open and startled to see Brian staring down at him.

"Not appropriate, Gabe?"

"You're fine, buddy. I left the door open for you."

"Are we ready?" He saw Joy asleep. "She needs to get up. We need to get dressed."

Closing the door behind them, Gabe said he would wake her up later. "Are you going to wear a tux, Bri?"

Insulted, Brian reminded Gabe that all the band members were wearing a tux and he played triangle in the band. William had rented him a tux, and he was going to wear it. When the time came, Gabe helped him, tying his bow tie after he was dressed.

Joy admired her guys, and they were effusive in their appreciation of her look. She wore her hair piled up, with tendrils hanging down. Gabe gave her his arm, and when she took Brian's hand, she noticed it was sweaty. Gabe handed her one of several handkerchiefs he had secreted on his person, and they took the elevator. He reminded Brian about all the people, with Brian agreeing he would be appropriate. But as soon as they joined the throngs, Brian announced in a loud voice that he saw, "Lots of boobies."

Hap and Megan had joined them, and Hap cautioned Brian to lower his voice. Then, turning to Megan, he asked, "Aren't you glad you didn't buy the green dress now?"

She blushed and nodded. "Didn't Joy say he has innocent eyes?"

"Good description. Yes, she did. And may I say you look perfect?"

"Thanks, Daddy. And so does Joy."

"She does, and so does your mother."

Walking beside them, Monte led them to their seats. "How's he doing?" he asked Joy, nodding toward Brian.

"Other than loudly announcing how many 'boobies' he sees, he's doing fine."

He chuckled. "Gotta admit, he's right. And you look lovely." He turned and shook Gabe's hand.

"Where's William and the guys? Are they late?" Brian stood and looked around. Catching sight of Rocky, Stan, Dave, and William, he waved madly. "I see them!"

When the Master of Ceremonies stood up, Gabe cautioned Brian to be quiet, reminding him if he could not be appropriate, they would have to leave. Brian immediately sat back down. The presentations dragged on too long for the lad, and Gabe pulled him onto his lap. When it was time for Joy's song, Brian quietly followed beside his brother. William directed him to his place beside the drums, pointing to where his triangle hung. Gabe took a deep breath, cautioning him to listen to William, who said, "I've got this, Gabe."

Gabe took his initial position behind Joy, and then they stepped up together and sang "Winslow Farm," hearing Brian's appropriate chimes behind them. They filed off the stage, and Brian took his hand, boasting, "I did good, Gabe. I did."

"You did perfect, my man." Brian reached up his arms, and William carried him down the stairs, off the stage. The boy rested his head on the drummer's chest. A photo of it in the next morning's papers captured the essence of the evening.

Joy won a Dove Award, and Brian cheered loudly but appropriately. While she conducted interviews, Gabe took Brian up to the room, and Brian was asleep when she came in. She went into his bedroom and kissed his cheek, whispering how well he had done. He did not even stir.

"I can't believe this! I hope Dr. Wells watched. He was amazing tonight. You were amazing, Joy. How can I ever thank you for what you have done for Brian?"

"I'm not the one with wings, Gabe." She turned her back. "Unzip me, please." She walked to their room and stepped out of her dress. "I can't tell you how tired I am." She barely had her nightgown on before she was asleep. He was content, stroking her golden curls and watching her.

* * *

At eight o'clock the next morning, Gabe answered the door. Joy and Brian were still asleep. Monte was there with an itinerary in his hand, containing schedules, appointments, and places to be. "Her first interview is in an hour. Where is she?"

"She's asleep."

"I told her last night we had to be up and at 'em early."

"She's pregnant—feels fine, but fatigued."

"You're kidding. This is a bonanza! Where's the coffee?"

"She can't drink it."

"Well, I can. Can you get her up?"

Gabe went into the bedroom and found Joy getting ready. "Monte told me you have a full schedule today."

She ran a brush through her golden curls. "I'll be ready in a sec. I hear Brian."

"Don't overdo it, baby. You need to think for two now."

"I know. Thanks, Gabe. Go check on Brian."

Brian was already up when Gabe returned to the living room. The boy asked, "Did you know Joy is going to have a baby?"

Gabe glared at Monte. "Yeah, I know. We weren't going to tell you until later, though. Nine months is a long time to wait, buddy."

"But I should know."

"We were going to tell you, Bri."

Joy came into the room, dropped a quick kiss on Gabe's lips, told him her dad would be by to take him hunting, and breezed off for her meetings. Hap knocked on the door a mere ten minutes later, but Brian and Gabe were already dressed. "Martha is fixing breakfast for you guys."

They left, and Hap told them they would be hunting at Stan's family farm. He thought it was too late in the day for hunting, but Stan told him deer were all over the place. Last year, with Brian sticking to him like glue, Gabe had a disappointing season, getting only one small deer. He anticipated a repeat, but he was surprised when his brother wanted to stay at the house and bake cookies with the sisters, Megan and Grace. Skipping breakfast, Hap and Gabe left, with Brian bragging he would have cookies for them when they got back.

Gabe, Hap, and Stan headed to each of the best hunting locations Stan knew. Gabe held his hand up and pointed, having spotted a deer, and Stan told him they could get closer. But Gabe brought his borrowed rifle to his shoulder and picked off the lone buck from across their vast distance apart. Stan and Hap stared in amazement, but Gabe seemed unaware.

Stan started walking back to the four-wheeler, saying he would drag the buck to the yard and hang it. He urged them to continue. Gabe was jubilant and eager to shoot another. Before Stan could return, he heard another shot, and he found Gabe and Hap dragging deer behind them. "I'm never going hunting with this guy again. He shoots them before I even see them!" Hap complained.

Gabe shrugged. "I hope you guys have tags."

Stan clapped him on the shoulder. "We have plenty. Dad always buys for my brother, and he never hunts. I wish he'd been here this morning—that was some fantastic shot!"

"You should have seen the second one," Hap said, describing the more recent shot, with Gabe revealing how pathetic his last season had been because Brian was so clingy. They hung the deer, gutted them, and returned to the hunt. Gabe continued walking around with Hap and Stan, and he pointed out a group of does, urging Stan to take a shot.

"Dude, I can't hit it from this distance," Stan said. Gabe shrugged and managed to move them closer to the deer. Hap took a shot, wounding one. And Stan finished her off.

"I'll take her back," Gabe offered.

Before he got to the yard, his phone rang. Martha told him he needed to get home because Brian was having a meltdown. "He did fine making the cookies, but he's been asking for his brother ever since." Gabe could hear him crying, and he castigated himself for not staying with him.

"Let me talk to him." Gabe told Brian they had bagged three deer and could leave some venison in Martha's freezer. But all Brian wanted to know was when he would be home. Once the girls finished making the cookies, they had drifted off to other

127

activities, and Martha only had "girl books" for Brian. Gabe told him he was with other people and did not know when he could be there.

As Brian grew more despaired, Joy returned. Gabe heard her comforting Brian, and soon, her voice came on the line. "We had a short night's sleep last night, Gabe, and both of us are tired. I rescheduled two interviews. We're going to take a little nap. We'll be fine, won't we Brian?"

Hearing his brother return to sniffs, Gabe responded he "owed her one." She playfully said if she could get a nap in, she might take him up on that offer.

Stan and Hap had finished for the day. The sun was getting high, and they already had two trophy bucks. Gabe wasn't interested in hanging deer heads on his wall, so he offered them to Stan and added he would be happy to share the meat as well. When they heard about Brian's meltdown, Stan urged Gabe and Hap to go back, saying he could finish up the butchering on his own.

Back at the Thomas home, Gabe peeked in at the two people he loved most in the world lying in bed, smiling to see Brian's arm draped around Joy and her arm tucked securely around his little brother. He cracked the door open a bit more to show Hap. "I'm blessed she loves him so much."

Hap agreed. "She's a loving soul. That's why her music touches so many—she gets it."

"She sings what we feel." Gabe soundlessly eased the door shut. "I guess we're stuck here another day. She quit early because she was so tired."

"Stan told me Brian's birthday is tomorrow. Maybe we could have a party for him tonight. Stan's neighbor has some retriever pups ready to go home, and he thought that might be a good gift."

"Brian wants a dog, and we sure could have used one recently." Gabe sat with Hap and Martha, enjoying another cup of coffee. He told them about his parents' death and the trauma that created the bond between him and his brother. "Joy is the first person he related to, other than me. And now he adores William, too." He described the scene in the kitchen when Joy cut the "dreadful" locks and how his brother had laughed. "I hadn't seen him laugh like that since before our mom died. Joy thought he was having a convulsion, and I was grinning like the Cheshire Cat."

The Winslows enjoyed the rest of the day at the Thomas's house. Martha was thrilled about the baby—her first grandchild. When they discussed names, Brian insisted it must be a girl. When Gabe asked him why, he said he did not want the baby to be difficult like he was. Gabe reiterated that he was not difficult, only inappropriate sometimes. But Brian insisted a girl would be better. Joy hugged him. "I like you exactly the way you are."

That evening, when the band members trooped in with presents for Brian, Martha brought out the cake she had baked when he was asleep, and they sang the birthday song. William gave him the triangle from the Dove Awards, Rocky gave him a band hoodie, and Dave gave him a band T-shirt. Stan scooted in beside the birthday boy and showed him a picture of the retriever mom and her pups. "Would you like to pick out one of these?"

"Oh, wow! Can I, Gabe?" Gabe grinned with a nod, and Brian threw his arms around Stan. They could go the next morning when Joy was at her interviews.

After Hap took them back to the hotel, and they went through the family ritual of saying Psalms 23, 91, and the Blesseds, Gabe did not even attempt to collect on Joy's earlier promise of allowing him to "owe her one." He was ready to sleep as much as Joy and Brian were.

* * *

The next day, Joy wanted Gabe to come along to her interviews, but he insisted he could not accompany her because he was not going to leave Brian. She was the star, after all. Nevertheless, Monte said they were learning Gabe was in demand, too, and he insisted Gabe absolutely must come.

"Brian had a meltdown yesterday. I can't leave him again."

"Bring him along, Gabe," Monte further insisted. "He'd break down a lot of stereotypes—as he has mine and several of the band members'."

Gabe shrugged. "I can always take him outside."

Not only was Gabe popular at the interviews, but so, too, was his little brother, who stole the show. Brian talked about William and the "dreadful" locks and about Gabe thinking it was not appropriate to love his boss, adding he was glad he changed his mind, because he loves Joy. He even asked an interviewer if she knew that married people need privacy. But that question almost got him removed. As for Joy, she described discovering Gabe's musical talent, and Brian reminded her that he told her Gabe could play the guitar. "I should have listened to you, Brian." Joy hugged him.

One of the taped interviews later had over two million views on YouTube, going viral. Gabriel Winslow could play the guitar, sing, and write songs. But it was Brian Winslow who stole the show, changing many people's stereotypes about youngsters with Down syndrome.

Several of the magazines interviewing them ended up wanting to do feature articles. Gabe, a private person, though not a true recluse as Joy once wondered, was reluctant. But he saw the advantage of giving publicity to Down syndrome children. So, with Dr. Wells's permission, he allowed his brother to continue being interviewed. The boy was overjoyed at a family photo of them that later appeared on the cover of one of the more popular magazines.

With the interviews over, they collected their new pup, a cage Gabe bought, and a bed Hap and Martha bought. They managed to get a ticket for the dog to fly, and they left on a Wednesday afternoon. When they landed, they collected their bags and the dog, and they let her out to use the bathroom. When they arrived home, Brian and the dog played until they were both tired. The beautiful pup crashed in her cage while her new family thought about names, finally deciding on Golden Beauty, but calling her Beauty for short.

When Beauty cried in the night, Brian sat up in his bed and rubbed his eyes. "What's wrong with her Gabe? Is she going to die?"

"No, buddy. She needs to go outside. Dogs don't like to mess in their space, so we need to take her outside. She'll train fast."

Gabe scooped up the pup and took his brother's hand. They walked outside and watched her do her business. Gabe praised her effusively, explaining to Brian they needed to teach her. After tucking the boy and his dog into bed, he snuck in beside his wife. Perhaps he should have waited until after their baby arrived before he got Brian a dog. But when the boy and the retriever became inseparable and played constantly, he knew it was a good thing.

CHAPTER 15

Back to School

BRIAN WANTED JOY TO go to school with him on his first day back. The special ed kids came in for orientation a day early, and he initially headed to his old classroom. Dr. Wells had told them he would be in a new room that year, but change was hard for Brian. Gabe explained this to Joy, so when she walked into the old room, she said, "Oh, Brian, this room looks too small for you. Remember Dr. Borchert said you'd grown so much this year when he did your physical? Gabe said you have a new room this year; we need to look for it."

Gabe should not have been amazed at his wife's expertise. She knew how to guide Brian. Maybe this year it would not be so difficult for him to make changes.

Dr. Wells stuck his head in the door. "I didn't see you in your new classroom, Brian. I thought maybe I'd find you here."

"Joy told me I'm too big for this room now."

Dr. Wells put his hand on the boy's shoulder. "She's right. I'll show you to your new room." Brian took the doctor's hand and followed him, with Joy and Gabe trailing behind. Joy talked to Brian's teacher and brought Brian into the conversation.

By the time they left, they had claimed Brian a desk, put his name on it, and made friends with his teacher, who seemed taken with him. Dr. Wells had notified her about the family's fame, and he asked her to keep it confidential, though she whispered that she loved "Winslow Farm" and had picked up the magazine with the family's photo on the front. Dr. Wells suggested that since Brian had become less shy about new situations, perhaps in a week or so they could try the bus. He further noted that the special ed kids' driver in their area was a super guy and that Gabe could ride on the bus with Brian for a few days while he tried it out.

"Thanks, Joy. You've opened new horizons for my brother." Gabe held the door for her.

"I haven't done anything except to love him."

"Mom loved him, too. But maybe she didn't expect as much out of him as you do. He seems to be rising to your expectations."

"Okay, we can go." Brian took Gabe's hand.

"Yes, boss. Where to?"

"Chick-fil-A."

"My favorite place, Brian." Joy took his hand. "Ready for school to begin?"

"Nope."

"Why not?"

"I want to stay home with Beauty. Why can't I stay home with you and Beauty? I need to practice the triangle."

"You can do that after school, Bri." Gabe led him down the long stairs in front of the school, urging him to hold the railing so he did not fall. Holding hands with Brian, with him in the middle, the couple dashed across the street to the parking lot. As usual, Gabe buckled him in, and as they drove, Joy and Brian sang. Gabe winked at Joy, signaling her to watch his brother tapping out the rhythm.

They always went inside Chick-fil-A, instead of doing the drive-through, so they could hear the music. Brian held hands with Gabe and Joy and reminded them he was too big for the play area. When they sat, Gabe tucked a napkin under Brian's chin. "What did you think of your new teacher?"

"She's nice. Not as nice as Joy, but she's okay."

"We're family, Brian. I'm your sister now."

"Yeah, I'm glad."

Joy hugged the boy. "Me, too, honey."

"Me three. I'm glad Joy married us, Bri."

"And now we're having a baby."

"I guess we need to add another bedroom to the cottage," Joy realized.

"Listen, Joy; it's our song."

"Winslow Farm" came on over the radio. Some people noticed them and smiled at the youngster. He was oblivious, though, as he mimed playing the triangle during his part.

* * *

In the following days, they settled into a new routine. Gabe took Brian to school for two weeks, and at the beginning of the third, the special ed bus began stopping in front of their house. Joy held Brian's hand and walked him to the bus to meet the driver. He was the first one on the bus, and the pleasant driver patted the first seat behind him. Brian asked Joy to say the Shepherd's Psalm, which she did, and the driver joined her. The boy beamed, telling Joy he would be okay with this driver.

Gabe was astounded at the good report—Brian had never ridden the bus before! The couple prayed for him, and they had no calls from the school except for Dr. Wells reporting Brian had gotten to his new classroom and liked his bus driver. All was good.

In the afternoon, Gabe and Joy met Brian at his bus, with Beauty snapped to a leash. Gabe shook the driver's hand and helped his brother get down the steps, listening to the other kids saying goodbye, with Brian calling back to them. Brian spotted the poles and the tackle box in Gabe's hand. "Are we going fishing, Gabe?"

Gabe looked up at the sky. "Is it going to rain?"

"Is it?"

Gabe held his hand out. "Don't see any clouds, do you? Do you feel rain?"

"No. It's sunshine."

"Then let's go!"

They drove the truck to the stream, and Joy even fastened her own worm on her hook. After fastening Brian's worm and tying Beauty's leash to a tree, Gabe sat behind Joy with his legs around her. The breeze rustled leaves softly overhead, and the stream gurgled happily. Life did not get any better. His brother was doing well, his wife was beautiful and loved him, and she was growing his baby. After what had at one point seemed unbearable pain, a new joy had seeped into his life—Joy-joy. He dropped a kiss on her cheek, and she turned to him with her brilliant smile.

"Oh, I think I got one!" Her bobber went down in the water. Gabe moved fast to catch Brian's pole as he flung it to the side to "help" Joy. The fish got away, and Gabe instructed her to jerk the line to set the hook next time. Brian hooked the next one, reeling it in and measuring it carefully then throwing it back. Beauty barked, and Gabe figured they would not catch anything else, so he sat with his hands across his knees. They watched two hawks push their babies out of a nest, making them fly. Joy was fascinated.

"That's what we are doing with you, Brian. We are pushing you out of the nest and teaching you to fly. Are you flying?"

"But you'll always come home to us, buddy," Gabe reassuringly added. "Every night, we'll be waiting for you."

Joy did set her hook the next time, which was a good thing because she battled one of the biggest fish Gabe had ever seen in their stream—definitely big enough to cook for supper. They stayed long enough for Brian to catch a keeper, too. It was technically too small to save, but Gabe put it on the stringer anyway.

"What did you do while I was in school?" Brian climbed into the truck, and Gabe buckled him in his seat. Joy's face flamed, and she turned aside. Gabe's face was flushed, too, as he thought about their day relishing their privacy. Joy had noticed, however, that he kept the phone right beside them all day in case the school called.

"Oh, we mostly lay around. Didn't get too much done. I'm working on a song about Joy. It's called 'You Make My Heart Break.'"

"Joy would never make your heart break!"

"When I looked at her at our wedding, she was so beautiful she made my heart break."

Brian frowned. "Is that okay, Joy?"

"He means it as a compliment. He means he thinks I'm beautiful. Isn't that silly?"

"No," the brothers chorused. And Gabe slapped Brian high five.

They went inside, and Joy started the grill while Gabe cleaned

136

the fish. Putting them on a screen, she salted and peppered them and then squeezed lemon. She breathed deep, drawing in the smell of the cooking fish and listening to it sizzle. It was a typical day on Winslow Farm.

Gabe and Joy helped with homework. Brian was good at math but struggled with reading comprehension, and Joy promised to read with him every night, which she did. Every night, before bedtime, Brian snuggled up to her. Gabe listened to her read *Black Beauty*, *Robinson Crusoe*, *Leatherstocking Tales*, and even *Little Women*, and she talked about each book as she read, increasing Brian's understanding. By the end of the semester, his reading comprehension had more than doubled.

* * *

After Christmas vacation, Gabe answered the phone. "Yes, take him to Stonewall Hospital in Weston. We'll meet him there." He looked at Joy. "Brian's hurt, and they're taking him by ambulance to Stonewall. Let's go." He hurried to help Joy with her coat and grabbed his own.

When Gabe's cell phone rang in the car, he spoke to the EMTs in the ambulance, who asked him to calm Brian. "Hey, buddy, can you hear me? Brian, it's Gabe. Shh, Bri. We're coming to the hospital. Yes, Joy is with me. We'll meet you in the emergency room."

Joy entered the conversation. "Hang on, kiddo; we're on our way. We don't have a siren, but we'll be there soon. Where do you hurt?" She learned he had a big bump on his head from falling on the playground. She kept him talking until the EMTs rolled him out of the ambulance, with Gabe and Joy turning in soon after.

Seeing Joy was pregnant, the hospital staff did not allow her to go into X-rays with Gabe and Brian, nor did she accompany them for Brian's CT scan. She only rejoined them when they moved him into a room where Dr. Borchert watched him for concussion symptoms. Dr. Borchert woke him every two hours, and Gabe and Joy remained with him the rest of the time. He would not tell them exactly what happened, just that he fell. He did, however, murmur something about "not tattling" and "only wimps tattle."

Gabe was concerned. Some older boys were in Brian's new classroom—bigger boys, with learning disabilities. "Let me tell you about being on a team, buddy. It takes everybody doing his part on a team. You need to think about everyone else. Sometimes it's necessary to tell what happened so someone else on the team doesn't get hurt, too."

"Did you ever tell, Gabe?"

"I sure did. Once in Afghanistan, I thought a guy was giving up our position, and I told my boss. He watched him, and, sure enough, that's what he was doing. If I hadn't told, we could have all been killed."

"Okay, so sometimes you tell?"

"Protect the team, buddy. What happened?"

Brian avoided looking in Gabe's eyes but replied. "Jim tripped me, and he picked up a rock and hit me." He pointed to the big bump. "Right here. But he said if I tell, I'll be in big trouble."

A muscle ticked in Gabe's right cheek. "Don't worry about it, buddy. We'll take care of it."

"Okay. I don't want to be in Jim's class, but I like Mrs. Stacy."

Looking down at his phone, Gabe told Joy he had a text from

Dr. Wells and would have to go outside to call him. Joy sat on the edge of the bed and held Brian's hand.

Stepping outside the hospital, Gabe told the psychologist what he had learned, and they agreed to check out the situation. He returned to find Dr. Borchert in Brian's room. "I'm urging her to go home. You can stay here with Brian, but she should rest. The nurses must continue waking him every two hours."

Joy protested, saying she could not rest. Gabe assured her that he had cared for Brian for almost a year without her and could care for him now. "Go fix some chamomile tea and let Beauty out." He wrote down the hospital room phone number for her to call, drew her close for a hug, and told Brian, "Send Joy home to rest, buddy. She needs to take care of the baby, okay?"

Blinking back tears, Brian held out his arms. Joy held him. "Can I wait until after he eats?"

"It gets dark early. I'd rather you go now."

"Call me if he needs me. Promise?"

"I will. We'll be fine, won't we, Bri? And we'll probably be home tomorrow."

"Wait, the baby is telling him goodbye." Placing her hand over Brian's, she put it on her belly for him to feel.

His eyes got wide. "I feel her, Gabe. Come feel her." Gabe rested his hand on her belly as well and smiled as he felt the flutters. She put her hands on his cheeks and brought him down for a kiss.

"One for you, too," and she gave Brian a kiss before she left.

Joy went home, but she could not eat a thing. She did drink the chamomile tea, though, and called her dad to tell him to pray. Hap prayed for Brian and for Joy, assuring her Gabe was right and asking about her well-being. She told him how Brian had felt the baby move, and she asked about her mother and sisters. She then called the hospital and talked to Gabe. As she listened to the low rumble of his voice, she realized she probably should have known earlier he could sing; he had a musical cadence to his voice, though maybe he had honed it singing with the band.

She was surprised she fell asleep after she tucked Gabe's pillow next to her face, breathed in his scent, and sang "You Make My Heart Break." He made hers "break," too, especially with his tenderness toward his brother. She wondered if she would have fallen in love with him if he did not have Brian. She smiled, remembering William teasing her about her "stud-man." She sighed. *Yep, he was a stud.*

She got up twice to pee, remembering Gabe teasing her about peeing for two. She easily fell back to sleep each time, and at 6:00 a.m., she rolled out of bed eager to go to the hospital. She did not want to call, in case they were asleep. But as she was dressing, Gabe called, saying it was likely they would be coming home soon. She told him she was coming, and he said they could not get Brian back to sleep, so he was going to hold him in a chair for a bit. Already on her way out the door by then, Joy slipped on her coat and braved the cold.

When she arrived at the hospital and looked into the room, she saw Gabe with his arms—*and wings!*—around Brian. His wings were lovely, soft, and strong. She took a deep breath and wondered if they would show up in a photo. Somehow, she doubted they would. But she saw them, and she could hardly wait to tell Brian.

Gabe stirred and looked up, his wings softly retracting into his body. "Hi, you. What are you looking at?"

"You. Did you know William teased me about my stud-man?"

"Who? Not me."

"Yes, you. I slept on your pillow last night and breathed in your scent."

"Oh come on!"

She stepped up to him and encircled him in her arms, feeling for his wings. They were no longer there. "I love you, Gabriel."

"Hey, don't wake the kid. We just got him back to sleep." With the tenderness she knew so well, Gabe tucked Brian into bed and turned to take her in his arms. "You break my heart, Joy. You taught my heart to sing, and you made me live again."

"I thought it was *Brian* who turns you into mush, not me."

He put Brian back into bed and then led Joy back to the chair and sat her on his lap. She nestled her head on his shoulder. She did turn him into mush. "I'd kiss you, but I fear my morning breath will slay you," he joked.

"I'll risk it. I missed you last night. I don't like sleeping without you."

"I believe that's our next song." He kissed her. "Or how about 'Kiss Me Awake?'"

"You are a veritable song machine."

"It's because I love you so much."

Hearing the breakfast trays coming down the hall, Gabe stood to open the door. Brian struggled awake, and while the orderly set the tray on his bedside table, Gabe took him to the bathroom. As the boy returned, Joy heard Gabe brushing his teeth, and she chuckled. She helped Brian into bed, put his napkin under his chin, and asked if he would like her to feed him. Nodding yes, he whispered, "He folded his wings around me when I was going to sleep. You saw them, didn't you?"

"I did. He was holding you in his lap, and his arms and wings were around you. How do they feel?"

"Strong. Soft. Comfortable." He smiled, and she wiped a bit of egg dribbling from his mouth.

"I'd love to feel them, but maybe they are only for you."

"The baby will feel them."

Coming out of the bathroom, Gabe asked, "What are you two whispering about? Christmas gifts are over."

"But your birthday is coming up." Joy winked at Brian.

The hospital discharged Brian later that day. Gabe, as usual, tenderly fastened his brother's seatbelt. "Where are we going to build the new bedroom for the baby?" he asked. "What do you think, Bri?" Gabe turned on the wipers to push away snowflakes falling on the windshield.

"In our old house, not the cottage . . . if we added a room for me downstairs."

"You didn't like sleeping upstairs?"

"It was so far away. I wouldn't be difficult downstairs. I'd give you privacy. I didn't like sleeping upstairs with the foster kids, being so far away from Mama and Dad. I want to be near."

"Dr. Borchert said you need to be home until Monday, so let's go home and draw up some plans. Is that okay?"

"Is Joy safe?"

"She's right behind us in her car. And it's not slick out."

They went home and made hot chocolate, drinking it while sitting around the kitchen table discussing plans. Since the cottage was only built for two, it had become crowded with Joy there. But Brian was comfortable in his old home now, and, logically, they felt they should move back there. They determined they needed to add three bedrooms—one for the baby, one for Brian, and another for the next baby. Joy's only stipulation was they must hire builders, though Gabe could oversee the project.

The baby wasn't due until April, but Joy could remain with the brothers at the cottage while they completed the renovations. Because of the weather, they were only able to start doing some prep work on the foundation, extending it. The temperature rose enough in March to pour concrete. Then cold socked in again, delaying construction.

Joy's belly swelled, but she was tolerant of Brian constantly wanting to feel the baby move. When Gabe fussed at him to quit, Joy insisted he should bond with his niece. He rolled his eyes but made no further protests, only asking if it drove her crazy. No— she thought it was sweet.

CHAPTER 16

Martha Ann

JOY WOKE HER HUSBAND on April 16. Her bag was packed, they had a room at Stonewall Hospital where Brian could be with them, and Gabe shook him awake. Brian ran to check on Joy, who urged him to get dressed in comfortable clothes because having a baby takes a long time—he might want to sleep. On the way to the hospital, Gabe could tell each time a contraction hit Joy, because she would rub her hand on her belly. He pulled up to the emergency room and went to get a wheelchair. Brian walked beside the orderly, promising to take care of Joy, while Gabe parked the car.

By the time Gabe arrived inside, Joy was gowned, and she was resting on the birthing chair. Brian had attended some of their classes and knew to expect Joy being in pain. She never cried out, though. Gabe rubbed her back, and Brian dozed. The nurse woke him in time to see his niece's arrival, but the blood sent him into a panic. Joy had never raised her voice to Brian until now, commanding him sternly, "Don't you leave me! Don't miss this, Brian. I want you to see your niece. Come here." She extended her arm to him.

He stepped into her embrace. "Don't die, Joy."

"Feel me squeeze your hand? 'I shall not die but live to recount the wondrous deeds of the Lord.' I'm having a baby. I'm not dying."

When the doctor commanded her to push, she grunted hard and pushed. Gabe wiped her brow as the doctor repeated his urging, and soon, they heard a wail. "She's a beauty, Mom." The doctor placed the baby on Joy's belly. Joy's legs were shaking, but she had a huge smile on her face. Brian reached out a tentative hand but then pulled it back.

"You can touch her, Bri." Gabe's hands encircled Joy's, and he shifted to give his brother room to look.

"She's greasy."

The nurse laughed. "We'll clean her up before you hold her. Right now she needs to feel Mommy's skin. Look, she's looking around for her." Joy brought her baby up to her breast and gently touched her cheek. The newborn instinctively turned and latched on. "Good girl," the nurse praised.

Gabe helped the nurse move the baby to the other breast, but soon, the nurse removed her altogether. Brian followed the baby to the table, where she protested a bit when she was wiped clean and wrapped in a blanket. A little hat covered her head. "So she won't be cold," the nurse explained.

"Joy won't die?" Brian asked. "It's a lot of blood."

While an aide sat Gabe in a chair and took the baby to him, the nurse took Brian's hand and looked straight at him. As usual, he avoided eye contact, but she put her hand on his shoulder. She explained that God built a nest inside of Mommy to protect the baby, and once she was born, Mommy did not need the nest anymore. The nest was mostly blood, and now it was coming out. Joy would bleed for a week or so, but she would be fine. The nurse assured him it was a normal thing—that all mommies bleed after their babies are born.

"Okay." Brian returned to Joy's side.

She was dozing, but her eyes fluttered open. "Hey, Uncle Brian." She greeted him. "Let him hold her, Gabe."

"You want to hold your niece?" Gabe stood, and the nurse put pillows around Brian's arms before Gabe gently lowered the baby down. "I'm sorry we didn't explain more of what to expect, Bri. I should have known the blood would frighten you."

"*I'm* like a big brother now."

"You are. How does it feel?"

"Okay. Good. Is she okay? She's quiet."

Gabe chuckled. "You wait."

The baby was born about six o'clock in the evening, and Joy was starving. The staff soon brought in three trays. Joy left not a crumb, but Gabe pushed his yogurt over to Brian. The baby stirred, and Gabe changed her. While Brian complained about the smell, the baby complained about where her milk was, and Brian suddenly realized his niece does not sleep all the time. Brian was fascinated watching her suckle, but he was self-conscious and averted his eyes.

"You'll get used to this, Brian." Joy assured him. "I'll have to feed her like this for at least six months. It doesn't bother me that you watch. I'll cover myself if other people are around, but you are family."

"Is Mom coming?" Brian wondered, referring to Martha. "Will you cover for *her*?"

"Mom and Dad are coming. They are on their way. I watched Mom feed my sisters, and they are family, too."

"Okay."

Dr. Borchert came in to check the baby, and the baby objected. She was poked and prodded. The doctor looked at her ears and put drops in her eyes, pronounced her a healthy baby, and said they could go home anytime. While a nurse wrapped the baby up, the doctor filled out the birth certificate—"Martha," for Joy's mother, and "Ann," for Gabe and Brian's mom. Settled back in her mother's arms, Martha Ann immediately began rooting around. "Go ahead and feed her," Dr. Borchert urged. "Has your milk come down?"

"Yes, and I feel swollen."

"That's good. Bring her into the office in six weeks. Call me if you need me in the meantime. Do you have help?" Learning Joy's mother was coming, he bid them good-day and exited.

Everyone was dozing when Joy's folks pushed open the door. Martha washed her hands and picked up the sleeping baby, crooning over her. She drew Brian next to her while she held little Martha. As was usual with everyone but Gabe or Joy, he averted his eyes, but he nevertheless hugged her.

Hap kissed Joy, shook Gabe's hand, and peered over his wife's shoulder. "She's Martha, after Joy's mom," Brian explained to an already-aware Hap. "My mama was Ann, and that's her middle name. Joy is bleeding, but she won't die. Mama died, but she didn't have a baby. She was hit by a truck."

"Tell me what our mom thinks about her namesake, Bri. That's what you call someone who is named after someone else."

"She's happy, Gabe. And Dad is, too, because Martha won't be difficult, or inappropriate."

Gabe pulled Brian into his arms. "I bet she's happy that little Martha has the best uncle ever, too."

"Yeah, Gabe. And you're the best daddy ever."

147

"He's talking about you, Brian. You're the best uncle ever." Joy's eyes swam with tears.

"Gabe is the bestest."

"Thanks, little brother. You're special, too."

Joy's mom lowered herself into the seat Gabe had vacated and examined every inch of her granddaughter, checking out her fingers and toes while Hap sat on the chair's arm. "Gabe, can you help me to the bathroom?" Joy held out her hand. When they came out, the nurse was there to help get the baby dressed. While Gabe and Hap went to get the car, Joy sat in a wheelchair, and the aide rolled her to the door.

"She has Gabe and Brian's dark hair and your curls," Martha observed.

"She's beautiful, Mom."

"She is. And here they are."

Hap got Joy into the car, and the aide checked that the baby was secure in the car seat. Joy sat in the back beside her, and Hap and Martha walked to their car, hand in hand. They stayed for two weeks, doing laundry in the house but fixing most of the meals in the cottage.

Gabe was glad to be back in his bed, and he did not mind helping with the baby one bit. Brian wanted to hold the baby often. And when she was asleep, he spent time in the house with Martha. "Do you think Martha Ann will look like Joy? Joy looks like you. You are both pretty."

Martha hugged Brian and almost got him to look at her. She tipped his face up and kissed his cheek. "That is a nice compliment, sweetie. I hear you are adding on to this house. I'm glad you'll live here. No ghosts, only lots of happy memories, right?"

"Gabe is building a room for me downstairs. But I'll be appropriate. I won't go to their room, because they are married, and you shouldn't disturb married people. They might want to plant a seed."

Hap raised his eyebrows, and Martha choked backed her laughter. "What do you want for dinner?"

"Can you make spaghetti like Joy does? Gabe makes it out of a can. I like it much better when Joy makes it."

"Spaghetti it is. Let's start the sauce now and let it simmer. Can you get the tomato sauce out of the pantry?"

"Martha Ann doesn't cry very much, does she? When she cries, Joy nurses her and she's happy again. Sometimes she needs her diaper changed. Gabe can do that."

"Gabe is a big help to Joy."

"Sometimes she cries, but he talks to her, and she looks at him."

"Do you want to see if the baby is awake now? Grab some noodles from the pantry, Hap. And bring the sauce when you come."

"I'm not missing time with my granddaughter either. I'll be right behind you."

The three of them walked back to the cottage and found Joy nursing the baby. Hap sat beside Gabe at the table, looking at drawings for the planned addition. "We'll put the baby's room beside ours, Hap. And we'll put a new bathroom on the other side of the master bathroom. Brian's room is next to it. Joy wants another baby, in time. She's a natural-born mother. I fell in love with her because of her goodness to Brian. But I said that to William once, and he said it didn't hurt that she's gorgeous, too." Gabe grinned.

"Brian said she looks like Martha."

"She does. He even told me he likes Martha because she looks like Joy."

Martha Ann began to cry, and Gabe got up to change her. Leaning over Joy, he kissed her cheek and took the baby. They had a changing table and some diapers in the corner, and Brian watched intently, twisting up his face when she had to have her butt wiped. "Ugh, Gabe! How do you do that?"

"I think about how uncomfortable she feels." He smiled at the baby. "Don't I, sweetie?" She attempted to return the smile. "Look at that. She'll be smiling back at us soon!"

"Can I hold her now?"

Gabe picked her up, and she belched. Everyone giggled, and Hap commented that she was not very ladylike. Joy piled some pillows on the couch beside her, patting a place beside them for Brian. Gabe lowered Martha Ann into her uncle's arms and watched him cuddle her with tenderness.

"He doesn't seem the least bit jealous," Hap whispered to Gabe.

Brian heard him and confirmed, "Oh, no, Pop. She's my baby niece. Gabe is her daddy, and he's my brother, so I'm her uncle."

"Got it all figured out, don't you, Brian?" Hap said. "How is Beauty doing with her?"

Hearing her name, the retriever moved over to where Brian sat, and she sniffed the baby. Joy pulled her over and rubbed her ears. "We told Brian he has to give her lots of attention, so he plays with her."

"I like Beauty. She was my best birthday gift ever, huh, Gabe?"

"And you take good care of her. Tell Stan thanks for us, Hap." Gabe snapped his fingers, and Beauty came over for a pet.

"Megan has seen a lot of Stan since the hunt. He showed her how to make jerky that very afternoon, and he helped her can a bunch of meat. That was how it began with those two, and she loves Stan's farm, too. Maybe we'll have another wedding this summer, Mama."

"Our girls are leaving us, Hap."

"So far their choices are good ones. Grace has taken a fancy to Rocky. She'll probably travel with the band. She's working toward a degree in music management at Belmont University. When I retire, maybe we'll all move back to Lost Creek. Could you spare a couple of acres on the farm, for us to build? That is, if you can tolerate all the Thomas family crowding you, Gabe."

"I'll already have the band members headquartered here permanently. All except for Stan, that is, who will go back to Nashville, to his family farm."

Martha Ann began to sir, and Joy took her. "Why don't you give Beauty some attention, Brian? I think I'll nap with the baby. When is supper, Mom?"

"Whenever. You guys rest. Were you up with her a lot last night?"

"A couple of times."

"You rest, too, Gabe. Hap and I will sit on the deck with Brian." Martha stood, and Hap followed her out.

* * *

Hap and Martha left after two weeks. Martha almost got Brian to hold her eyes before she left, but his inevitably skittered away. They had good times in the kitchen, though, and she felt she had made progress with him.

After Martha and Hap's visit, Brian went back to school with photos of his niece to show everyone. The addition to the house was completed, and, true to his word, Brian stayed in his room at night and never bothered Gabe and Joy after going to bed. Each night, the family recited the 23rd Psalm, the 91st Psalm, and the Blesseds, and Gabe kissed him on the cheek.

One night, Brian heard his brother up with the teething baby. He peeked into the nursery on his way to the bathroom. He was right—Gabe's wings were out and were nestled around Martha Ann. He could hardly wait to tell Joy the next morning. It would always be their secret.

Gabe worked on the farm that summer. Thank God they did not need anyone to work the perimeter anymore. By mid-summer, they were ready to work on their next album, and the band returned. Martha Ann seemed as taken with William as her uncle was, and she patted his brown cheeks with her fat little fingers. He would catch them in his lips and kiss them, and she would giggle. William kept his hair short, but not as short as Gabe's.

Grace worked on her Belmont degree, which was a year away. The band did a tour at the end of summer, and Megan traveled along to help with Martha Ann. Rocky missed his gal, and their phones hummed constantly. She decided to go to summer school so she could graduate in December. They married on December 28. Gabe walked down the aisle with Joy, leaning over to whisper, "You do make my heart break, Joy. You are so beautiful."

She turned her beautiful smile on him and whispered, "I love you, Gabe."

The next spring, Gabe and Joy had a little boy. They named him Bruce, after Gabe and Brian's father. He was not difficult, just energetic. And Brian loved him.

CHAPTER 17

Brian Grows Up

BRIAN ENTERED MIDDLE SCHOOL that fall. Gabe taught him to use deodorant, and, if he forgot, Joy reminded him. "Have you brushed your teeth, Brian, and put on your deodorant?"

Gabe rarely held Brian in his lap anymore—he had gotten too big. Brian felt the wings less, and he missed them. He told Joy that once he outgrew Gabe's lap, he outgrew his wings, too. But he was glad Martha Ann and Baby Bruce still felt them. He held his niece and nephew whenever they needed cuddles. Always loving, Brian enjoyed giving them affection. He even learned to hold Martha's eyes, and from there he graduated to holding the eyes of others, including his teachers.

Another baby joined the household when Bruce was three, and they named him Michael—another angel. They had three children now—Martha Ann, Bruce, and now their other angel. Michael was Gabe's clone, with dark hair that tended to curl and dark, piercing eyes.

When Brian got to high school, he became interested in a girl. She was another Down syndrome child. Gabe cautioned Brian about being too affectionate. Sometimes it was not appropriate in a boy–girl relationship, Gabe explained—it could lead to planting a seed.

Gabe spoke with Brian and a doctor about preventing pregnancy, but Marlene remained Brian's love-interest. Her parents appreciated Gabe's devotion to Brian, and they confided to him that they had gotten Marlene's tubes tied, fearing the same thing Gabe did. She, like Brian, was sweet and affectionate, and they did not want someone taking advantage of her, knowing she could in no way care for a baby. The sweethearts were content to just hang out with Gabe, Joy, and the children, and they were committed to each other. Marlene was from a Christian family as well, and Gabe emphasized his concerns by making sure the couple understood that sex outside of marriage was a sin.

"Okay, Gabe. We'll wait. But I want to marry Marlene when we graduate." Brian took her hand when he said that, and she murmured her agreement.

One Friday night, Marlene stayed late, with no word from her parents. Joy made her welcome and told her she could sleep in Martha Ann's room. Brian asked if Marlene could come in and join them when they read the Psalms and said the Blesseds, which she did, saying, "I liked that. I'll sleep better tonight."

"Gabe started to read them to me when I was in grade school, after Mom and Dad died and he came home to live with me. I love you, Gabe."

"I love you, little brother." Gabe kissed Brian's forehead, and Joy led Marlene to her bed in Martha Ann's room, across the hall. Marlene asked if Joy would kiss her like that, and Joy placed a gentle kiss on the girl's forehead.

Gabe and Joy were reading in their bedroom when her phone rang. Gabe could hear background noises coming from the phone as Joy spoke into it. "It's no bother. Stay with the team. We put her to bed in our daughter's bedroom. . . . Oh, no, I don't think of it like that. She's a sweet young lady and no trouble at all. We consider all our children blessings, including Brian. He's Gabe's brother, but I fell in love with him when we first met. Let her stay the night whenever they have a home game—no problem. They played with Brian's dog and the children."

Joy set her phone down none too gently. Gabe raised his eyebrows. "What's got you so upset?"

"That horrible man!"

"Marlene's father?"

"Yes. He apologized that he left his 'little accident' with us so long. He said he knows she is a 'bother.'"

"She does ask questions constantly."

"She wants to learn. Brian and Marlene are like Martha Ann and the boys—'Why this? Why that?'"

"Martha Ann is six, and the boys even younger, Joy. Brian and Marlene are teenagers. Some people have trouble understanding that."

"Children are God's gifts. When I was first getting to know you and Brian, I asked God if Brian would be perfect when he gets to heaven. You know what He said?" Gabe shrugged. "He said He thought Brian was pretty perfect now. And he is. He has a child-like innocence. Marlene does too. When we grow up, maybe we can be like them."

"You are a wise woman, Joy Winslow. And I love you." He kissed her again, clicked off the light, and showed her how much.

* * *

The band remained intact. Stan and Megan and Rocky and Grace had married into the family and began to add their own children. Martha was a wonderful grandmother, and she always made sure Brian knew she considered him her first grandchild. William got married as well, to one of the backup singers who came to the farm whenever they were working on songs and cutting digital masters. Brian was always "my man" to him and played the triangle. William met Marlene the summer after her and Brian's sophomore year, and he pronounced her a "great catch," which pleased Brian to no end.

"Be sure I get an invitation to the wedding, my man."

"All the band will be here for it. We'll get married in the living room, where Joy and Gabe were married."

"We may have outgrown the living room, Bri. How about the church?"

"Okay. But we are getting married."

"I got that, little brother."

"You need to drop that 'little brother.' He's as big as you, Gabe."

"Not quite. But he'll always be my little brother. Right, Bri?"

"Okay. Will you sing at my wedding? You and Joy?"

"If you want."

"Sing 'Winslow Farm.' That would be good."

At graduation, the Winslows sat with Marlene's family and demonstrated how to celebrate enthusiastically when the two of them got their alternative degrees. They took them out to dinner, with Joy ably handling Brian and the three children—Martha Ann, Bruce, and Michael. Brian had learned to tuck his napkin into his shirt front, and he helped Marlene with hers.

Two weeks later, Brian and Marlene were married. Gabe had built them a big bedroom with a living area and a bath plus a little kitchenette on the end of the house. The band threw them a big shower, and everyone had a grand time. They toured with the band, with grandmother Martha and now-retired Hap traveling along to take care of Joy and Gabe's three children and Megan and Stan's one. Grace and Rocky were expecting.

Martha's cup was truly running over. She and Hap were torn about moving back to Lost Creek, with their two younger girls still living in Nashville. Gabe agreed to Hap's solution of giving the grandparents a couple of acres behind the house, where he built a small cottage for them to stay whenever they were visiting, including when the band was in town.

After the band finished its last tour performance, in Colorado Springs, Gabe and Joy walked beside William and his wife. William glanced aside to where Brian and Marlene walked. "Hey, I see a little tongue in there." William nodded to the couple. "Where did he learn that?"

"From the master," Gabe replied, drawing Joy into his arms.

"I remember the day when she said she wanted you to be more than a guitarist, and we told her Brian said it was inappropriate to love your boss. She said she *wanted* you to be inappropriate, and we asked what she meant. She meant she wanted you to kiss her. I guess you figured that out eventually, seeing as you two came out of her room with her cheeks whisker-burned."

"I never could resist his kisses. Maybe there should be a song about it." Joy leaned into her husband's arms. When they went back to the hotel, Gabe got out his guitar. A song was born that night, and Winslow baby number four was born not long after.

* * *

Martha and Hap drove to Winslow Farm before the baby was born. They wanted to see their new cottage while they were there. Fortunately, it was almost complete, and they were able to stay there. Martha told Joy they were saints to include Brian and Marlene in their family. "Brian I've always adored, but Marlene is not as high-functioning. She drives me crazy, I must admit."

Joy chuckled. "But *Brian* adores her. And isn't it sweet?"

"I guess. But now you have another baby coming. How will she be with Faith?"

"We'll see. God works all things together for our good, because we love Him, and we are the called, according to His purpose. Marlene's father called her his 'little accident' and said she was a 'bother.' I was furious! Imagine disdaining God's gift like that! He was all caught up in her older brothers' sports and totally ignored her. We are so blessed to have her. We didn't hesitate to include her here."

"Gabe is an amazing man, Joy."

"He is, and that's why we have number four coming any day now." She rubbed her belly. "The day I bought Winslow Farm was the best day of my life. I had no idea I'd find a guitarist and a songwriter, but I loved him and Brian right away."

"And I love them, too." Martha hugged Joy and felt her daughter's belly tighten. "How long has this been going on?"

"A couple of hours."

"Honey, this is your fourth—she will come faster than the others. We need to get you to the hospital. Where's Gabe?"

"He's over at your place, with Daddy. I'll call him."

Within minutes, Gabe arrived, grabbed her suitcase, kissed

Martha, exhorted Martha Ann, Bruce, and Michael to be good for their grandmother, and tucked his wife in the car. Martha was right—Faith was born only two hours later. "You've done it again, Joy. You've given me another beautiful baby, and this little one looks exactly like you."

"We have a houseful. I need to start resisting those kisses."

"Never!" Gabe changed Baby Faith and handed her over to Joy, helping settle the little one on her mama's breast. "The kids are all coming over this afternoon. Hap is driving the van."

"Bless his heart. You'll have to go out and stay with the kids so Mama can see the baby."

"They are waiting until after Brian and Marlene get home from their jobs. Brian said they could stay home today in honor of the occasion, but Martha encouraged them to go."

"She told me Marlene drives her nuts and that we were 'saints' to take her in. I told her about Marlene's father. Brian and Marlene can't live independently, so we had to bring her in. She told me what a good person you are, Gabe."

He leaned to kiss her. "And don't you forget it," he teased, with a wink, taking the baby out of her arms and carrying her to the bassinette to change her. The baby immediately closed her eyes. "Need to go to the bathroom?" He helped Joy attend to that.

Gabe sat beside Joy's bed, and they talked about her parents' cottage. He said they decided on a kitchenette because they figured they would eat their meals at the main house. Before long, Joy drifted off. Gabe wished for his guitar, thinking about a song—"You've Done It Again"—and the beautiful wife who loved his brother and gave him his family.

Martha and Hap herded Martha Ann, Bruce, and Michael into the room. Hap jerked his thumb toward the waiting room. "Marlene is nervous about seeing the baby. Brian's calming her down."

The children gathered around the infant. Martha Ann wanted to hold her, and they arranged pillows for their ten-year-old daughter to hold her baby sister. She had already agreed to share her room with Faith when the baby outgrew the bassinette in their parents' room, so they gave her first privilege. Martha stood beside her namesake as they remarked together over Faith. The boys took interest, too; especially Michael, who was four and was a sweet, calm child, like a mini-Gabe. He observed his sister with the baby and noticed how much the baby looked like their mother.

After everyone had kissed Joy, they filed out to let Gabe's brother have a turn. "If you don't want to come, I'm going without you," Brian told his wife. "Faith is the only one I wasn't with when she was born, and I want to see her. Come on." He reached for Marlene's hand, and she followed. "Oh, Joy, she is beautiful. She has your golden curls. Look, Marlene." Because he had been so good with all their children, Gabe allowed Brian to pick up the baby and hold her close to his chest. When her tummy gurgled, and the air was laden with an unpleasant odor, he handed him up to Gabe, who grinned and took her for a diaper change.

"Ugh! What is that smell?" Marlene gagged.

"It's just mu . . . muc . . ." Brian looked at Gabe.

Gabe supplied, "Meconium."

"Joy's milk is cleaning her out," Brian asserted confidently. He was an old hand at this baby thing.

Marlene grabbed tissues and held them under her nose. "She stinks."

"Once she's cleaned out, her poops will smell sweet. Won't they, Gabe?"

Expertly fastening her diaper, Gabe grinned. "Until she starts eating solid food."

"How can you change that?" Marlene wrinkled her nose.

"Gabe says he thinks about how uncomfortable she is. Right, Gabe?"

"That's right. We were all babies once and needed someone to help us." Thinking the better of offering to help Marlene hold the baby, Gabe tucked her into her mother's arms instead. "You two help Miss Martha with the children, please."

"Okay." Brian led Marlene out the door, looking back with longing at Baby Faith. Martha stuck her head in to say goodbye, and Joy promised her when they got home she could hold Faith to her heart's content.

As soon as Gabe and Joy were alone with the baby, Joy suggested they pray for Marlene, and they did. "Brian may have to keep her in their place much of the time in the evening, but at least they'll be at work all day," Gabe pointed out.

"He is so good with the babies, Gabe."

"He is. We'll see how it goes. But his wife comes first."

"I never had to share you with anyone."

"You always shared me with my brother. Thank you for loving him. Do you need to nurse her before I put her down?"

"No, I need to rest." Joy laid her head back and closed her eyes, but her lips were moving. Gabe knew she was praying, and he rocked Faith. Before Joy's eyes closed completely, she saw Gabriel's wings surround her new baby. She smiled in contentment.

* * *

They brought the baby home on Saturday. All the kids were on the back deck, and Michael shoved a bouquet of wildflowers into Joy's hand. Hap unbuckled the car seat and handed Faith to Martha, who immediately took her to the rocking chair in the living room. The children gathered around her. Martha Ann and her grandmother sat together, and eventually, the boys drifted away to play with Beauty in the yard. Brian and Marlene went back to their space, but Brian returned, saying his wife was taking a nap. "She was the youngest in her family, Joy. She's not used to babies. Can I get you anything? Water?"

Gabe sat on the footstool in front of Brian's chair. "We understand, Bri. You've taken a vow to forsake all others. Marlene is your wife, and she comes first."

"But we want you to know Faith. You are good with babies, Brian." Joy's eyes swam. "Come here." Brian stood beside the bed, and she lifted her arms. "I love you, Brian Winslow."

"I love you, Joy. Thanks for . . . for loving us—Gabe and me. You're the best thing that ever happened to us."

"You got that right, buddy." Gabe cocked his head. "Sounds like Faith needs her mama."

"She does." Martha came across the room. "Do you need anything before you nurse her?"

"Brian will bring me a glass of water."

Martha turned and saw him. "Hi, Brian. Is Marlene all right?"

"She's taking a nap. She was the youngest—she's not used to babies. We won't have any babies. Her parents had her fixed."

"Well, I'm glad you have one another."

"Me, too." Brian stood to get Joy's water and brought it back.

He put a napkin on the table beside the bed before setting it down. "Anything else, Joy?"

"You might check on the boys. They're in the yard playing with Beauty."

"Okay."

"Where are Dad and Gabe, Mom?"

Martha had claimed the chair Brian left. "They're down at our place, inspecting the garden window the contractors put in today. And Martha Ann and I are going to bake cookies." She looked up. "Ready, Martha Ann?"

"I got out sugar, and butter, and eggs."

Martha stood. After kissing her daughter and caressing Faith's golden curls, she turned back to her granddaughter. "Did you turn on the stove?"

"No, ma'am."

"We'll do that before we get the flour and chocolate chips. We need to make peanut butter cookies, too. They're Brian's favorite."

A while later, Gabe entered the kitchen sniffing the air. "Hey, Martha. Made Brian's favorites I see. Yum." He grabbed a cookie off the plate. "Where is he?"

"Joy sent him out to oversee the boys playing with Beauty."

"I'll check on him in a minute." Gabe peeked in on his wife and baby in the bedroom. Faith was scooched up in her bassinette, and Joy was sound asleep. The baby's little bottom stuck up. *Good to see Joy sleeping. She didn't get a lot of sleep last night. Thank you, Lord, for this woman.* He picked up his guitar and went to the living room, where Martha Ann joined him. "Did you help Grandma with the cookies, Martha Ann? They're mighty good." His daughter sat beside him on the sofa, and he put his arm around her.

"Mama's asleep. I looked in on her a minute ago."

"I saw. Shall we go check on the guys?" They went out onto the deck and found Beauty with her head resting on Michael's lap while Brian and Bruce were digging for worms.

"Hi, Dad." Bruce greeted him. "Brian and me thought we could go fishing later."

"Maybe, if you can manage by yourselves. I hate to leave Mama on her first day back home."

"I thought Grandma could look after her."

"She and Martha Ann made you some peanut butter cookies. But be quiet—Joy and Faith are asleep."

Michael patted Beauty and ran to the kitchen with the rest of the boys. There, Hap dropped a kiss on Martha's cheek. "Did you teach Martha Ann how to make these?"

"We had a fine time. She's a good helper."

"You're a wonderful grandmother. If I had known how wonderful grandchildren are, I'd have started with them first."

She chuckled. "We are blessed with wonderful sons-in-law."

"I'll never forget Gabe taking care of all of us during that ordeal here."

"He's a good man and a good father. But I love Rocky and Stan, too."

"Our daughters chose well."

The kids came rushing in and swarmed the plates of cookies. Martha told them to leave peanut butter cookies for Brian because they were his favorite.

"We have plenty to share, Grandma Martha," Brian chimed in. "Marlene likes the chocolate chip better."

"Is she at your place?"

"Yeah. She's not used to babies. I like babies."

"You've always been good with the babies. Hasn't he, Hap? You wanted a girl when Martha Ann was born, but the boys aren't too bad, are they?"

"They're not difficult. Dad said I was difficult. Gabe did, too, one time. But I give them privacy now."

"I can understand that. And Martha and I will leave them to their privacy, too, before long."

"Okay."

Gabe and Joy joined them as they moved back to the living room. Faith was asleep in the bassinette, and Joy was eager to sample the cookies. She had one peanut butter and one chocolate chip, pronouncing them both delicious.

* * *

The baby slept four hours most nights after Martha and Hap left. Grace's baby was due in Nashville the following month, so they were gone by the time Marlene had a meltdown. Gabe was walking Faith, who had cramps and was crying. Marlene kept telling the baby to be quiet, and she raised her voice each time, eventually adding in a loud voice, "Shut up!"

Feeling the baby respond to the tension, Gabe told Brian to take his wife out of the house. "Do whatever you have to do. Make her a cup of tea. Make love to her. Just get her out of here, please." Brian led Marlene down the hall to their room, leaving the wide-eyed children behind.

Martha Ann was troubled. "What's wrong with her, Mama?" She asked. "It's more than just she's not used to babies."

"I agree. Let's pray for Marlene, kids."

"She shouldn't talk to our baby like that," Bruce insisted.

"Every baby cries."

"I know what's wrong with Faith. She probably has a little gas," Martha Ann added. The baby let out a roaring belch, and her sister asked, "That was her problem, wasn't it, Daddy?"

"Mama's right. Let's pray for Marlene." The family sat together and asked God to help Brian's wife with Faith.

"It's not fair. Brian loves the babies, and Marlene is spoiling it for him. What's wrong with her?"

"God will show us, Martha Ann. Now get ready for bed. Tomorrow we have church."

Joy rocked the baby while Gabe put the kids down for the night. When he returned, she was putting Faith in the bassinette. He shut their door and took her into his arms. "You're such a good mother."

"I was a mother the first year we married."

"You told me you wanted to make a baby with me."

"I did. I mean, you're so much older than me." Joy's eyes twinkled as she teased him.

He huffed. "Not *that* much older!"

"I know. You're perfect, and I love you."

They heard a tap on the door, and Gabe answered it, finding Brian standing there. "Am I being difficult?"

"No, Bri. What do you need?"

"Can we talk?"

"Sure." Gabe followed him out to the living room, and Joy trailed behind them.

Brian dropped his head. "Before Marlene's family moved here, she was . . . Some guys, three of them, did bad things to her. That's why they got her fixed." He raised his head. "She was crying, and those guys told her they'd comfort her, and then they

166

did bad things."

"Oh, Brian. I'm so sorry." Joy comforted him.

"She was so scared that we couldn't, you know . . . do it, after we got married. I just held her." He wiped his eyes. "She was just so scared. That's why her parents moved to Lost Creek. Our first time was in Colorado for the concert."

"In Colorado? That was over a year later!"

"Yeah. It was hard. I had . . . you know . . . needs."

"Oh, Brian, what a sweet sacrifice," Joy said. He shrugged.

"Is it better?" Gabe hoped. "Is it good for you now?"

Brian grinned. "It's good, since you told me to rub that nub in the front of her legs until she got wet, Gabe. I was real gentle, like you said. She really likes that."

"That's good. I'm glad for you."

"Me, too." Brian looked away. "I'd like to kiss her there. Do you?"

"That's private, Bri. It's between you and Marlene. You must do what pleasures both of you," Gabe counseled him.

"So I just ask her?"

"Yeah, that'd be good to do."

"Okay."

"I'm sorry to be difficult. She's not afraid anymore, but she got upset when the baby was crying. When Marlene cried, that's when it happened to her. That's when the boys did bad things to her. I wanted you to know."

"I'm glad to know. Thanks for telling us, Bri. And we'll pray to be able to help her."

"Okay." Brian stood, and Gabe took him in his arms.

"God will reward you for waiting and being patient. You are a good husband."

"It's easier now."

"I bet."

"Okay." Brian turned and went down the hall to his room.

"'Night, Bri." Gabe chuckled. "He took my advice. Did you see his pajama pants were on backward?" Joy grinned, and Gabe sat. "Can you believe that? Over a year. I couldn't even wait one night, though I offered to."

"I didn't want you to wait. He's the sweetest person I ever met."

"Yeah. I remember in Colorado he asked me what women like, but I never dreamed he wasn't getting any."

Joy stretched out her hand. "Come on; you want to kiss the nub between my legs?" She playfully teased.

Gabe shook his head in disbelief. "I can't believe the things I've had to tell that kid."

"Just remember to put your jacket on before you plant a seed. It's cold in the garden."

* * *

The baby woke them before 6:00 a.m., so Gabe decided to make a nice breakfast. Michael was in the living room when Joy finished nursing, and she handed Faith over to him. "Hold her while I get dressed." In the bedroom, she suggested to Gabe that he call Brian and Marlene to join them. But when she opened the door, Brian was already standing outside it. He put his finger to his lips and nodded his head. She looked around him and saw Faith cuddled in Michael's arms, his little wings wrapped around her.

"Oh, Brian! We have another secret," she excitedly whispered.

Gabe crossed the room. "You two have had secrets from me

168

for years. What is it?" Brian turned toward the living room, and Joy put her hand on his forearm. "What?" Gabe persisted. Then, looking over their shoulders, he saw Michael and the baby. His mouth dropped open.

Joy whispered, "I knew Michael looked exactly like you, Gabe. But I didn't know he inherited your wings."

"My wings? What are you talking about?"

"We've seen your wings for a long time, Gabe. My first time was in the hospital after Mom died. You held me in the chair, under your wings."

"This is crazy!"

"And the first time *I* saw your wings was in the hospital when Brian had his concussion. But I've seen you with them with every one of the babies, too—Martha Ann, Bruce, Michael, and Faith."

"I don't believe this!" Gabe walked over to Michael, and Michael's wings receded. His father knelt in front of him. "Hey, little guy, are you okay? You want me to take her?"

Michael drew her closer. "No, Dad. I like to hold her. It makes me feel strong."

Gabe reached around to feel behind his son's shoulders. No wings. Was he seeing things?

"They go in, like folding up," Brian informed him.

Gabe looked over at Joy. "Really? So I wasn't seeing things?" Joy shook her head. "How often have you seen my . . . my . . . wings?"

"Oh . . . lots of times."

"When does it happen?"

"When you are tender."

"Tender?" he echoed. "Then have you ever felt them?"

"Not that kind of tender. I asked Brian what they feel like, and

169

he said strong, soft, and comforting." Gabe looked at Brian.

"I told Joy when I outgrew your lap, I outgrew your wings. I miss them."

Gabe stood and ruffled Michael's dark hair. "Guess I'd better get breakfast started. I hear Martha Ann up. Does she see them, too? Does anyone else see them?"

"I told you once, you have to have innocent eyes. Maybe the kids saw them when they were little. But no one else has mentioned it, other than Brian."

"And you."

"Yes, and me."

Bruce came hurtling into the living room. "You fixing breakfast, Dad? Can I help?" Gabe set him to making toast while he cracked the eggs and Joy put bacon in the pan. He kept stealing glances at Michael, to see if his wings reappeared. He didn't see them. The rest of the morning was uneventful. Marlene joined them for breakfast, and they all went to church.

* * *

Six months later, Joy finally felt Gabriel's wings. She had felt increasingly bad throughout the day, and Gabe took her to the emergency room. They were there until nine o'clock trying to get her blood pressure down. Finally, they gave her a shot. After running some tests, the doctors determined she would eventually need gallbladder surgery, and they reluctantly released her. By the time they returned home, Faith was crying, and Joy's breasts ached to nurse her. She winced when she picked Faith up, and she sat with her in the rocking chair.

Gabe lifted Faith out of Joy's arms and carried the baby to her bassinette before returning to the living room and putting Joy on his lap. He held her, and for the first time, he noticed his wings as they folded around her. Reaching up, she touched them. They were strong, soft, and comfortable. Mystified, Gabe held her until she started drifting to sleep. He stood to carry her into their bedroom and felt the wings recede.

"I've felt that before. So that's what it's been this whole time? It's my wings receding?"

A sleepy Joy looked up at him. "You reach around sometimes, like they might itch or something."

"This is crazy. But I've seen Michael's, so I believe it."

"Me, too." Joy held her arms up, and Gabe popped a gown over her head. As soon as he had his pajamas on, he crawled into bed beside her.

"Do you need a pain pill?"

"No, I feel great. She rested her head on his chest, and he stroked her golden curls, musing about the mystery of wings.

The next morning, Gabe began a word study on wings, starting with their favorite Psalm—Psalm 91, verse 4. "He shall cover you with his feathers, and under his wings, you shall take refuge." He looked over at Joy, who insisted she felt great and did not need the pain medicine. "Honey, where is it about healing in his wings?"

"It's in Malachi, the fourth chapter."

He turned and read: "But unto you who fear my name shall the Sun of righteousness arise with healing in His wings." He leaned his head back on the couch. "You feel okay?"

"I feel terrific—like I was never sick."

"Do you think this wings deal has anything to do with healing?"

"When Dr. Borchert checked Brian's head the day after he

fell and you held him, he asked where the bump was, remember? And usually, it happens when you're comforting the babies. And when Martha Ann had her sore throat, and I was getting dressed to take her to the doctor for a strep test, you were holding her, and I saw your wings then, too. She hopped down and felt fine. Then when Bruce fell, and we were sure his leg was broken, you held him on the glider, and I saw your wings. He ran off before long. So, maybe. Yeah—maybe healing comes."

"Remember when we prayed for Marlene and asked God to help us heal her fears? Well, maybe *this* is the answer. I just don't know how to turn it on and off."

"When you feel tender, hold her."

"But I don't feel tender when she carries on. I get mad, actually."

"We can pray about it."

Two nights later, the opportunity came. Faith was teething, and they were out of stuff to rub on her gums. Gabe was looking for Hap's brandy. But Joy insisted she did not want her baby to be drunk, and Marlene was becoming increasingly agitated about the crying again. Brian looked at Joy. "Pray, Joy. Pray for Gabe and Marlene."

Joy was glad she had confided in Brian, and she immediately began to pray. Marlene had her hands over her ears, getting more and more worked up. This time, Gabe had compassion when saw her. Joy sat to nurse the baby, while he put his arms around Marlene, and she felt his wings. She stared in astonishment, but he soothed her. "Shh, Marlene. It's okay." He walked over to the rocking chair, pulling her onto his lap, with his wings wrapped around her until her anxiety drained away. "Is that better?"

She nodded against his chest. "What did you do? What was that?" She reached for his wings, but they had receded.

"It's a secret," he whispered. "God touched you."

"Come on, Marlene. Let's go to our place." Brian held out his hand, and she took it and followed him.

"What happened?" she asked him. He shrugged. And Marlene never had another anxiety attack.

"So, what happened?" Gabe asked Joy when they went to their room. Faith stirred, and he lowered his voice. "We need to get this kid out of here. She's cramping our style in the bedroom."

"Your style is fine as is." Joy sealed her statement with a kiss.

"But I miss those whimpers you make. They turn me on! Wait, does a winged man talk like that?"

"You've been talking that way for years, Gabe." But they moved Faith into her sister's room the next day anyway.

CHAPTER 18

The Day Innocence Died

SEVERAL YEARS LATER, the band was due in, when the phone rang. "Mr. Winslow? This is the pastor from Horizons. Something has happened to Brian, and I have Marlene here." Gabe heard her sobbing uncontrollably in the background.

"Should I talk to her?"

"You need to come, quickly."

Earlier, Gabe had dropped Brian and Marlene off to walk the trail near the church. "I'll be right there." Gabe grabbed his keys, hollering to Joy that something had happened to Brian and that he was headed to the church. He took off, sensing the urgency. He pulled into the parking lot and heard Marlene as soon as he pushed the door open. Making his way to the pastor's office, he pulled her into his arms. "What happened?"

"They killed him!"

He sought the pastor's eyes and saw his sad agreement. "The police are gathering evidence. It appears some boys assaulted him."

Clinging to Gabe, Marlene added, "They were going to do bad things to me and told him to watch. He fought them. He said it wasn't going to happen again. He hit one boy, and they all

174

jumped him. One of them kicked him in the head. Why did they kick him in the head? I screamed and screamed, and they ran off."

"Several of us heard her scream, but when we got there, the boys were gone. Brian was dead before the EMTs arrived. I'm sorry, Mr. Winslow. I wish we had gotten there sooner."

Someone shoved a chair under Gabe. He sank into it, pulling Marlene onto his lap, whispering, "Shh, sweetie," as tears rolled down his face. *This couldn't be happening. It was a nightmare. How could he tell Joy?*

A knock sounded at the door, and two uniformed policemen stepped in, confirming all he had been told. They had cordoned off the area where the assault occurred, and they were gathering evidence. Numb with shock, Gabe agreed they could transfer the deceased to the funeral home in Jane Lew. *The deceased. His brother, Brian. Bri was deceased!* "I'll have to take her home before I can go down to make arrangements."

Someone shoved tissues into Gabe's hands, and he mopped his face. He managed to get Marlene into the truck, gently fastening her in the seatbelt and kissing her on the cheek, through her tears and his own. He stopped to bow his head and asked God to help them survive and help him tell Joy and the family. Thumbing his phone, he informed his own pastor, who agreed to meet him at the house.

The pastor arrived at the house shortly behind Gabe. Joy welcomed them, staring at the distraught Marlene and a broken-hearted Gabe. She steered them into the house, allowing Gabe to take Marlene into his lap as she continued to sob. Wanting to hold Joy, too, who loved his brother every bit as much as he did, he wept as he choked out the story. She sank beside him on the couch, shaking her head and whispering, "No . . . no." Gabe managed to get an arm around his wife and mingled her tears with his own.

The pastor called a doctor, explained the situation, and arranged for the doctor to bring a sedative. Soon, a nurse arrived. She gave Marlene a shot and left some tablets. Gabe carried her into the bedroom she had shared with Brian, leaving the door open. Martha Ann promised to listen for her while Joy, Gabe, and the pastor went to the funeral home. She was there when the band arrived, and she told them what had happened. William sobbed, Stan and Megan listened in horror, and Rocky and Grace made the call to Hap and Martha, who would start out for the farm immediately.

Gabe asked the funeral home to mask the bruises so Marlene would not have to look at them. He supplied Brian's suit, and they planned the services. The funeral director promised Brian would look nice, but Gabe bitterly responded that he would look dead.

When they got home, Martha Ann had kept Faith as content as she could with a bottle, but the baby was not happy until Joy nursed her. In tears, Joy mourned. The baby girl would never know her Uncle Brian. Marlene woke up, but she could not be enticed to eat. Her parents, who had been in Charleston for high school basketball tournaments, came by. They asked if she wanted to come home. She answered that her home was here, where she lived with Brian.

* * *

The next day, Gabe's phone rang, and he was surprised to learn it was The White House calling. *What in the world?* He affirmed he was Gabe Winslow, Brian Winslow's brother, and that, yes, his brother died of wounds defending his wife. Joy then heard him say, "Thank you, Mr. President," and briefly report what had happened. Speaking into the phone, he added that most Down syndrome individuals are guileless and affectionate. And that, often, they are aborted, but those who are not are very much in demand for adoption because of their disposition.

"My wife says this is the day innocence died. . . . Yes, sir, that would be wonderful, and I'll put you in touch with some experts." He knew Dr. Wells's number by heart, and he gave it to the president. "Right now, we are trying to hold his wife and ourselves together. . . . That's very kind, thank you."

Gabe hung up the phone and, looking around, said, "That was the president. He heard the news and called to offer his prayers and condolences. He saw us featured on several news programs after the Dove Awards and fell in love with Brian. I guess they're reporting news of Brian's death now. The president is going to declare a day of recognition for Down syndrome children in his name. Brian is still teaching and positively impacting people, even now."

People stood out in the street at the funeral home, waiting in line to offer prayers and love. The biggest basket of flowers came from the substitute guitarist, signed simply, "God knows I'm sorry, Dean." Gabe and Joy had directed that gifts be donated to education programs for Down syndrome children.

Gabe, Rocky, and Stan managed to keep Marlene upright for the service. Once home, Gabe and Joy fretted because she would not eat a bite. They prepared all her favorite foods, but she would shake her head and refuse. Then, on the fourth day after the funeral, she told Gabe she had dreamed about Brian and that Brian said to tell William he was standing on God's front porch. "What did he mean, Gabe?"

"You know how honest Brian was, right? A long time ago, when Brian was ten and Joy had recently met him, I told William how honest he was—how you always knew exactly where he stood. And Brian responded that he was standing on Joy's front porch."

"I want to stand on God's front porch with Brian."

Joy looked stricken. "Oh, Marlene, stay with us!" But she shook her head at Joy. They called her parents, informing them they could not get her to eat. They came over, and Joy was gratified to see them come to somewhat of a resolution with Marlene. Her dad comforted her by apologizing for favoring her brothers, but he had no success as far as getting her to eat.

Marlene was dwindling to nothing. Always chubby, she was now thin and wasted. Gabe enfolded her in his wings often, getting her to sleep. But she would not eat more than a morsel. Her parents agreed it was futile to hospitalize her for force-feeding. The doctor gave her appetite stimulants to no avail, and one morning, when they went to rouse her, she did not wake up.

CHAPTER 19

The Nest Empties

MARTHA ANN MOVED IN with her grandparents in Nashville while attending Vanderbilt nursing school, and Bruce followed in Gabe's footsteps, accepting an ROTC scholarship to Virginia Tech. Michael, Gabe's spitting image, was always aware of his wings and used them to comfort and heal others, but quietly and with circumspection. Several years later, he went to an Anglican seminary in Connecticut and was ordained into the priesthood.

Faith shared her mother's beauty and musical talent, and she went to Belmont University in Nashville to major in voice. They loved singing together, and they planned to join their voices at a Belmont production. They were on their way to the concert in Nashville when Gabe's phone rang in the car. "Dad?" Martha Ann asked from the other end, her voice strained.

"What is it, honey?" he replied.

"Are you in the car?"

"Mama and I are on our way to Belmont."

"Oh. Maybe you ought to pull over."

"I'll call you from the rest stop. It's about ten miles up. Are you okay?" Their daughter hung up without answering him.

"Something is wrong," Joy frowned, anxious to pull off.

When they pulled off to make the call, Martha Ann answered immediately. "Mama, it's Grandma. I came in from school, and she was on the floor in the kitchen. They've already taken her for an autopsy, but they suspect she had a brain hemorrhage. She didn't suffer, Mama."

Gabe pulled Joy into his arms and let her weep. Pulling herself together, she asked Martha Ann how Gramps was. "He's shocked, and he's sad. I mean, what can you expect? How far away are you? Stan's here with him."

"About another five hours, I'd say."

"Be careful, Dad. Nothing you can do now except comfort Gramps."

Joy did not want to stop for dinner—she wanted to be in Nashville. They pulled into the driveway about eight o'clock, noting Stan and Megan's car, as well as Grace and Rocky's. The family members clung to one another while Gabe prepared food. When Joy could not eat, he reminded her of Marlene. So she took a sandwich and some fruit salad.

What Martha Ann had heard was correct. Her grandmother had died of a massive brain hemorrhage. Holding her father's hand three days later, Joy said goodbye to her precious mother. After the burial, the family gathered in the Thomas's home, filling the place with laughter and wonderful memories. How good it was to know the Lord and His peace and presence. Somehow, Faith and Joy managed to make it through their rehearsals and their production at the university, with Gabe and Joy deciding to stick around afterward to comfort Gramps.

About a week later, Stan encouraged his father-in-law to take a walk and scout out some hunting sites. Gabe joined him in getting Hap out of the house, while the girls sorted out Martha's clothes. When Gabe returned a short time later, the moment Joy saw his face, she knew something was wrong. "It's Dad, isn't it? What happened?"

Gabe did not want to give her the news. How could she survive two blows at once? "He collapsed. Heart attack, I'm guessing. Stan said he'd get help. But Dad said he'd be fine—said he'd just 'go sit under that tree by Martha.' By the time Stan got back, he was gone. He was smiling, Joy."

"He didn't have the heart to live without her. They married when she was eighteen. He was twenty." She sighed and blew her nose. "We have to tell the girls."

For the second time in a month, the family celebrated the resurrection, burying Joy's dad. Once again, Michael preached a triumphant service. They were not surprised to learn the grandparents willed the family home to Martha Ann, who was planning to marry a doctor in the fall.

Joy, who was much smaller than her mother, only took a few of her mother's shawls. Some of the clothes fit Martha Ann, but Faith was small, like Joy. She only wanted a few afghans and mementos. The girls finished distributing things among themselves, and Gabe and Joy traveled home, to Winslow Farm.

* * *

The bittersweet sadness of the funerals somewhat dampened their favorite season. Joy and Gabe walked to the stream and soaked in the blessings of autumn as best they could. They cuddled in their bed, remembering the happy sounds of the house, while silence now echoed around them. But Michael established an Anglican church nearby, living in the former caretaker's cottage. And Faith married a fine musician—Andrew's baritone was deeper than Gabe's, but his voice blended with Faith's in beautiful harmonies, evocative of Gabe and Joy. They, too, gravitated to Lost Creek, moving into Brian and Marlene's old room, and the house filled with music again.

Eventually, Faith and Andrew added a kitchen to the cottage Gabe had built for Martha and Hap, and they settled there instead. Sometimes Gabe and Joy joined them in their music, but most of the time they were busy cutting their own music, backed up by their band members, who stayed upstairs when they were in town.

Stan and Megan stayed on his farm in Nashville. And Martha Ann and her husband, an orthopedic surgeon, both worked at Vanderbilt. Rocky continued to produce, and he and Grace helped launch Faith and Andrew's music career.

On the anniversary of Brian's death, now more than a decade ago, Gabe determined to shake off the seasonal melancholy by writing a tribute to his brother. They called the song "Standing on God's Front Porch." Gabe opened, singing, "My brother, Bri," and Joy joined in with, "Brian, my friend." It was to be their last Dove Award.

CHAPTER 20

A Tribute to Joy

GABE WAS CONCERNED about Joy's response to their travel for the Dove Awards. She had been thrilled to see Martha Ann and the Thomas sisters, Megan and Grace, but she tired quickly. When they got home, he insisted she see a doctor, and his fears were justified. She had cancer of the worst kind—pancreatic. When the hospital had done everything it could do, Gabe brought her home on hospice.

Joy was determined to see Michael marry the woman God had called to join him in his labors. Reminiscent of that day many years ago, they married in a quiet service in the parlor, with Joy remaining seated in a wheelchair. Faith and Grace prepared a nice celebration, but Joy pushed her food around. Seeing her fatigue, Gabe broke up the celebration early.

Once everyone had left, Gabe scooped Joy up and settled her in his lap, wrapping his wings around her. She always felt better for a while, but she never rallied. The hospice folks visited twice a week, knowing she was already tenderly cared for and that they could do little else. Michael and his bride visited every day and prayed with her.

One day, Gabe decided he would spend longer than usual

with Joy in his lap, his wings enfolded around her. They talked a bit, and she dozed. That afternoon, she wanted to go downstairs.

"I have a gift for you, Gabe. A goodbye present."

"You can't leave me, Joy. Remember, I'm much older than you."

She smiled. "You'll like it. God gave it to me." Gabe carried her downstairs. Once there, she stood on her own, behind a mic, and sang into it while it recorded her voice:

Many years ago, I made a vow: 'til death do us part.
But I rescind it now, 'cause in my heart I know,
death cannot our love sever.
I will love you forever.
I will hold you near to me,
keep you dear to me.
You will hear me whisper.
You'll know all I say, 'cause in my heart I know,
I will love you forever.

Joy held up her hands without a word, and Gabe carried her upstairs.

"Do you want to sit on my lap?"

"I'd like to lie down. Did you like it?"

Choking back his tears, Gabe told her it was a beautiful song—a perfect gift. He put her on the bed, and she pulled him down for a kiss, murmuring, "I will always love you."

The hospice nurse came and closed Joy's cornflower blue eyes, now faded. The nurse notified Michael, who arrived within twenty minutes. He called Martha Ann and Faith and her husband, who were all in Nashville. Bruce flew in from his duty station, and they laid Joy to rest on a hillside in Lost Creek. The crowd slowly drifted away, but Gabe remained there, immobile.

"It's time to go home, Dad." Michael took his arm.

"I need your wings, Michael." Michael wrapped his wings around his father. "I remember the first time I saw these."

"I was holding Baby Faith."

"You were. And Brian and Mama told me you had inherited not only my looks but also my wings."

"Was that really the first time you knew about our wings?"

"It was. But after that, I consciously used mine. They healed often." Tears streamed down Gabe's face. "Why didn't they work for Mama?"

Realizing Michael was ministering to their father, his siblings moved to their cars and headed to the farm. "Sometimes they don't, Dad. They are God's gifts, and they operate according to His will. My best guess is He needed Mama's voice in heaven's choir."

Gabe's mouth twisted into a rueful smile. "Probably true." He patted his son's arm. "We can go now."

* * *

All too soon, the adult children returned to their homes. Knowing Faith was expecting her first child, Gabe suggested that she and Andrew move into his and Joy's old room in the main house, and he would move into their place—the one he had built for Hap and Martha. They made the switch, and Gabe moved the bed he had shared with Joy for thirty-eight years. The young couple had their own bed, and Faith and her husband cheerfully painted and prepared a nursery.

Another grandchild—how Joy had looked forward to each

one. Martha Ann had two now, but Bruce was still a bachelor, with Michael only recently married. Joy had rejoiced to see the quiet wedding ceremony in the parlor. And Michael's wife, Bethany, was a lovely girl. Faith was expecting a girl, whom she insisted would be named Joy, after her mother.

It had been bittersweet having everyone at Winslow Farm after Joy passed. As usual, funerals brought laughter and celebration to the Winslow family—happy memories, poignant memories, and lots of laughter—as it should be in a celebration of life. Bruce had lifted his glass of iced tea, saying, "Here's to Mama, standing on God's front porch with Uncle Brian." And everyone else had raised their glasses in agreement. "Here, here!" And Gabe heard Joy quietly agree. *Did he hear her voice, or was it only what he knew she would say?*

Gabe silently blessed Faith and Andrew, praying for them to experience the love he and Joy had known. Gabe did not grieve, because he felt Joy near, seeming to hear what she would say in these moments. He was content puttering around the farm. He mowed the meadow, causing turkeys to rise and scatter. He remembered how excited Joy had been when she learned there were turkeys at the farm. "Remember, Joy?" he asked aloud. And he felt her smile. He abandoned his plans to continue mowing and decided to check the fence line instead. Although they had not had any repeat of the terrible events that required the razor wire to be strung, they had maintained the gate and the fence.

Faith continued in the entertainment industry, and she was every bit as beautiful as her mother—her spitting image. *Is that disloyal to you, to think that, Joy?*

No, she's my baby, Gabe—our baby. You had Michael, and I had Faith, and we both had all of them.

186

Gabe wondered what his children would think about him conversing with their dead mother. Maybe they would think he was in his cups at sixty-eight years old. But he did not care; he liked conversing with Joy. Real or imaginary, it was comforting. But if he could not mow, and if the fences were fine, what else would he do? *The decks need staining. Okay, I can do that*, he thought. He headed for the house.

He decided to check with Faith because the back deck was off her bedroom, but she was asleep. The funeral and the company had worn her out. He remembered Joy's pregnancy fatigue— Faith was so much like her mother. He decided to do the deck of the caretaker's cottage instead, because Michael and Bethany were out pastoring, visiting the sick and shut-in. Michael was a good pastor, and Bethany was a perfect helpmate.

Gathering up the stain and a few nails, Gabe walked to the cottage. He walked the smaller deck, remembering the day he added it, with Brian handing him the nails, one by one. He chuckled, and he felt Joy giggle with him. He thought about her gift to him—the song she sang the day she died—wondering if he should share it with others or whether it was his alone. Maybe he would ask Michael.

Later, he heard Michael come into the cottage, where he was now sitting. "Hey, Dad. Why are you sitting in the dark? May I turn on a light?" At Gabe's assent, Michael flipped a switch, flooding the room with warm light. "You're not depressed, are you?" Michael lowered himself into the chair next to his father's.

"No, not really." Gabe's Bible lay on his lap. "I feel your mother with me. We even talk sometimes, though I know that sounds crazy."

"You two were soulmates. Not only lovers, but you worked

together. You shared your whole lives. I guess you knew what each other thought most of the time."

Gabe set his Bible on the table. "I want to share Mama's last gift to me with you. She sang it the day she died."

Gabe rose and started playing the recording of Joy's lovely music. Without accompaniment, her voice sounded clear and true: "*I will always love you.*" He held his breath, but it was Michael who wept.

"How beautiful, Dad." He looked over at his father. "I know how you two always worked together, so where is your stanza?"

Gabe explained the circumstances. "She stood behind the mic and sang. I had held her in my lap most of the day. When she stood and belted it out, I thought maybe my wings had worked. But she deflated again after she sang, and she lifted her arms to me. I carried her upstairs. She wanted to lie down, and I knew she wouldn't wake up." Also without accompaniment, Gabe's voice now rang out:

The day we wed, I whispered and said,
"You are so beautiful, you break my heart."
And now we must part.
Again, you break my heart.
For *I will always love you.*

Michael held his breath and then jumped up. "Where is Faith? We need her and Andrew." He brought them in and played Joy's farewell song. And he urged his father to sing his new stanza. "We can record this and put their voices together, with their lovely harmonies."

"I don't know," Gabe cautioned. "I thought it was her gift to

188

me only—her farewell. But what do you think?"

"We should do this, Gabe," Andrew urged him. "It will be her legacy."

Faith could hardly suppress her excitement. "We should do this song, Dad. And then a legacy album! You could narrate the background of each song you and Mama wrote."

* * *

At the Dove Awards that year, Gabe sang on stage as they played Joy's voice in the background, blending their harmonies. He included his stanza, and the song closed with their harmony singing the refrain. Later, everyone said they felt Joy's presence on the stage with him.

After Faith and Andrew produced and recorded "Joy's Farewell," Gabe devoted himself to recording his narration of the backstories for each of Joy's songs. Because she had such a long and prolific career, even recording some songs before he knew her, he chose to begin the narration with the song she was singing when she walked into his heart, and he continued it from there.

Gabe spent time on each of their award-winning songs. He recorded the story of "Winslow Farm," reliving the agony of protecting Joy from a demented stalker, and "You Break My Heart," about the day they wed, and "Our Child," about Martha Ann. He also told the story of "Standing on God's Front Porch," recalling his ruthlessly honest brother, Brian, who told William they know right where he stands—on Joy's front porch. And he talked about how Brian later came to Marlene in a dream and asked her to, "Tell William I'm standing on God's front porch."

Even though Gabe devoted himself to nothing other than the narration project, it still required months to finish. He eventually called the project "Joy's Legacy," completing it over a year after it began. Several members of the band—William, Stan, and Rocky—also added narration. For example, Stan related Joy's desire for Gabe to be "inappropriate" by kissing her (his boss), mentioning her whisker-burned face when Gabe and Joy emerged from her bedroom.

"Joy's Legacy" ended up being six vinyl recordings and seven DVDs. Once Gabe was satisfied, "Joy's Legacy" went to market. Joy won a posthumous Lifetime Achievement Award, and soon after, Gabe joined her and Bri on God's front porch. Michael and the rest of their children celebrated at his funeral, though Michael preached the service with tears running down his face. They knew their beloved father was with the woman and the brother he had loved so well.

From the Publisher

Thank You from the Publisher

Van Rye Publishing, LLC ("VRP") sincerely thanks you for your interest in and purchase of this book.

If you enjoyed this book or found it useful, please consider taking a moment to support the author and get word out to other readers like you by leaving a rating or review of the book at its product page at your favorite online book retailer.

Thank you!

Resources from the Publisher

Van Rye Publishing, LLC ("VRP") offers the following resources to writers and to readers.

For writers who enjoyed this book or found it useful, please consider having VRP edit, format, or fully publish your own book manuscript. You can find out more, and contact the publisher directly, by visiting VRP's website: www.vanryepublishing.com.

For readers who enjoyed this book or found it useful, please consider signing up to have VRP notify you when books like this one are available at a limited-time discounted price, some as low as $0.99. You can sign up to receive such notifications by visiting the following web address: http://eepurl.com/cERow9.

From the Publisher

For anyone who enjoyed this book or found it useful, if you have not already done so, please again consider leaving a rating or review of this book at its product page at your favorite online book retailer. These ratings and reviews are themselves extremely valuable resources for writers and for readers like you. VRP therefore hopes you will please take a moment to share your thoughts about this book with others.

Thank you again!

About the Author

CHARLOTTE S. SNEAD holds a Bachelor of Arts degree in Psychology from Duke University and a Master of Social Work degree from the University of North Carolina. OakTara published her first three books: *His Brother's Wife*, in 2012, and *Recovered and Free* and *Invisible Wounds*, in 2014. Charlotte later received Jan-Carol Publishing's Believe and Achieve Award for her novel *A Place to Live*, the first of a scheduled five-book series. While working on the remaining books in the series, she also published her first children's book, *Deano the Dino Goes to the Doctor*, in 2018.

Charlotte married her husband, Dr. Joseph Snead, in 1962. They raised five children and a foster daughter and now proudly grandparent ten boys and one girl. One of their children and four of their grandchildren are adopted. Charlotte was the daughter of a career military officer, who served in WWII, and Dr. Snead served in Vietnam. Their son was a career military officer, so Charlotte has a special place in her heart for our military.

In keeping with Charlotte's strong belief in and celebration of the joys of marriage, family, and writing, she maintains a blog (at www.charlottesnead.com), which has the tagline "Sacred Passion—It's God's Idea." Please feel free to contact her there.

Made in the USA
San Bernardino, CA
07 March 2019